ARETE

ANCIENT WRITERS, PAPYRI, AND INSCRIPTIONS
ON THE HISTORY AND IDEALS
OF GREEK ATHLETICS AND GAMES

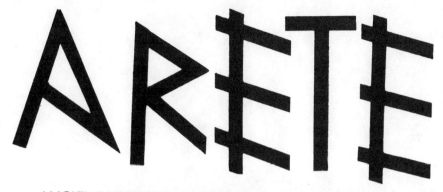

ARETE

ANCIENT WRITERS, PAPYRI, AND INSCRIPTIONS
ON THE HISTORY AND IDEALS
OF GREEK ATHLETICS AND GAMES

By
STEPHEN G. MILLER

ARES PUBLISHERS, INC.
CHICAGO MCMLXXIX

©1979
ARES PUBLISHERS INC.
7020 North Western Avenue
Chicago, Illinois 60645
Printed in the United States of America
International Standard Book Number
0-89005-313-8

INTRODUCTION

This book has arisen from a need to put into the hands of my students ancient readings which provide evidence for and reveal various aspects of Greek athletes. These students are, for the most part, undergraduates with no prior experience of Classics and the Classical world. These students are also, again for the most part, bright and eager and more than willing to confront the problems of a lack of evidence or of conflicting evidence from antiquity, but they do not have the ancient languages necessary to deal with literary and epigraphical evidence. This is, then the need which I hope that this book will fulfill, and it should be used together with a general handbook such as E.N. Gardiner's *Athletics of the Ancient World* which will provide a general background together with photographs and drawings of the physical evidence for the study of Greek athletics.

The only book which has been available for a need such as that described above has been R.S. Robinson's *Sources for the History of Greek Athletics*. Because of the use of some of the same sources, there are many similarities between this book and that of Robinson, but there are also many differences. First of all, I have omitted some of the material included by Robinson in her collection because I can find no purpose in its retention. At the same time, I have included other material which Robinson omitted. Some of this consists of more recently discovered epigraphic texts, some is material which I hope will make certain points about our view of Greek athletics. Secondly, Robinson's collection is organized chronologically, whereas this arrangement is thematic. Although this arrangement will make the evidence for certain specific problems easier to find, it also brings together evidence of widely different dates. The reader should always bear in mind that practices may have changed between dates of different documents. Thirdly, I have found

Robinson's work less than easy to use and potentially confusing, largely because it was set in a single type face which makes it difficult, at first glance, to distinguish between the ancient source and the modern comment. Finally, I confess that I find many of Robinson's translations unnecessarily flat.

Given the need from which this book has arisen, its thematic organization has been designed to augment and complement successive classroom lectures and discussions upon specific topics. Such a format and the sources selected for it are obviously highly subjective. Many of the sources are also clearly relevant to more than one topic, but the overall arrangement has been made with certain points, which are admittedly argumentative, in mind. The Table of Contents will at least reveal the nature of these points and I can hope that the reader will understand them and, perhaps, come to agree with them. I would have liked to have included many more sources, but athletics and athletes are so pervasive in the literature of antiquity that the final result would have approached the whole corpus of our extant Greek, and much of our Latin.

The translations are my own and will be recognized to be as idiosyncratic as the choice of the original passages themselves. I have tried to present readable, perhaps even enjoyable, translations with something of the flavor of the original but without doing violence to the meaning of the original. I have taken liberties, especially in poetry, for the sake of clarity. Thus, for example, in the Homeric poems some metaphors have disappeared completely, others have been put into a more contemporary idiom, and proper names have replaced pronouns and substantive patronymics. I have taken no liberties with technical terms, or with words which purport to be technical terms. I have simply transliterated these words, italicized them and attempted to give a definition of each in a glossary at the back of the book.

Inscriptions and papyri which are less than completely preserved present a special problem. I have tried to indicate, by the use of brackets, dashes, dots, etc., what is actually preserved on the stone or the papyrus and what has been restored by modern editors.

Many of the entries are provided with a brief introduction the purpose of which varies. Sometimes the introduction is intended to provide the dramatic background for the action described in the source, sometimes to provide pertinent information about the author or the document, and sometimes to indicate particular problems to which the source is relevant. The goal of these brief introductions has been always to aid the student in an understanding of the source and of its importance for ancient athletics.

Another problem has been with the translations of sums of money. It would have been simpler (and safer) to have transliterated them and to have given a general indication of the value of, for example, a drachma at different periods of time. But I have yet to find a student who is satisfied with such an explanation when the question is raised: "How much is that worth today?" My method, which has no guarantee of being correct, has been to take the daily wage of a skilled workman from the appropriate period of time (when we know it) and equate it with a wage today of $8 per day. This is admittedly very conservative. R. Scranton in *The Muses at Work* (ed. C. Roebuck, 1969), p. 26, suggested ten years ago that the rate might be set at $15 per day. My rate of exchange is, then, clearly not excessive, but the figures which sometimes result seem to be so. It is difficult at first glance to believe that, for example, Theagenes of Thasos (no. 43) could pay a fine of some $96,000 or that Demokedes of Kroton might be paid a salary of a like amount, but we are dealing with athletics to which large sums of money are not unknown even today.

My debts are many and I can hardly repay them here, but I must express my gratitude to R. Stroud for his steadfast encouragement, to Al. Oikonomides for his willingness to publish this book, and to my wife for her help, patience, and occasional *bon mot*. I would also thank the more than 200 private donors and the National Endowment for the Humanities who have made possible our excavations at Nemea which have, in turn, nutured my interest in Greek athletics. Finally, I would thank the nearly 200 students who have endured earlier versions of this book, and it is to them that I would dedicate this effort. May their successors benefit from their sufferings.

University of California
at Berkeley

Stephen G. Miller

TABLE OF CONTENTS

Patroklos, the childhood and lifelong friend of Achilles, has fought in Achilles' place and been killed by Hektor outside the walls of Troy. The corpse of Patroklos has been cremated and the crowd at the funeral begins to disperse:

But Achilles held the people there and sat them in a broad assembly, and brought prizes for games out of his ships, cauldrons and tripods and horses and mules and high-headed powerful cattle and beautifully girdled women and gray iron. First he set forth the glorious prizes for equine feet: a woman faultless in her work to be led away and a tripod with ears holding twenty-two measures for the first prize. Then for the second he set forth a six year old unbroken mare carrying an unborn mule foal. Then for the third prize he set forth a beautiful unfired cauldron holding four measures, still new and shiny. For the fourth he set forth two gold talents, and for the fifth a two-handled unfired bowl. Then he stood up and spoke out to the Argives:

"These prizes are placed in competition awaiting the horsemen. If we Achaians were not competing for the sake of some other hero, I myself would take the first prizes away to my tent. You know by how much my horses surpass all others in their *arete,* for they are immortal, a gift of Poseidon to my father Peleus who handed them in turn to me. But I and my solid-hoofed horses stay aside; such is the fame of the charioteer whom they have lost, the gentle one, who so many times rubbed soft oil into their manes after he had washed them with shining water. Therefore they both stand here grieving him with manes trailing on the ground, both hearts grieving as one. But the rest of you take your places in the field, whoever has confidence in his horses and compact chariot."

So spoke the son of Peleus, and the swift riders gathered. By far the first to rise was Eumelos, son of Admetos, who surpassed all in horsemanship. After him rose Diomedes, strong son of Tydeus, and yoked the Trojan horses which he had taken by force from Aeneas. Next rose fair-haired Menelaos, son of Atreus, and yoked his swift horses. Fourth to prepare his flowing-maned horses was Antilochos, glorious son of high-hearted king Nestor. He stood nearby and gave well-intentioned advice to his son:

"Antilochos, Zeus and Poseidon have loved you, though you are young, and have taught you all aspects of good horsemanship. Therefore, I have no need to instruct you, for you know well how to double the *terma*. But I think that your horses are the slowest, and that your work will be harder. The horses of these men are faster, but they do not know better than you how to plan. Remember then, my dear boy, always to have your plan in mind so that the prizes will not elude you. The woodcutter is far better with skill than with brute force; it is with skill that the pilot holds his swift ship on course though buffeted by winds on the wine-colored sea. Thus too by skill one charioteer passes another. But whoever puts his trust in his horses and chariot and recklessly turns wide coming and going, his horses drift out of the course and he cannot hold them. But the man who takes the advantage is he who, though driving the slower horses, always watches the *terma* and turns it tightly, nor forgets how much oxhide rein to give and take, but holds his horses well and studies the man in front. I shall give you a marker, and you cannot miss it. There is a dry stump about six feet high above the ground, either oak or pine, but not rotted by rain water, with two white stones against it on either side, and there the course is smooth around it; it may be the marker of some man long dead and buried, or the *nyssa* set up by earlier men, but now Achilles has made it the *terma*. Having approached this, you must drive your horses and chariot near it, and you in your well-woven chariot box lean toward the left; then call out to your right horse and goad him on, and give him full rein. Your left horse must be driven up close to the *nyssa* so that the hub of the wheel seems to touch, but do not let it graze the stone lest you harm your horses and break your chariot. That would be a thing of joy for the others and a source of shame for you. My dear boy, keep your wits about you and be careful, for if at the *nyssa* you drive hard and slip ahead, there is no one who by sprinting can catch you, let alone pass you."

So spoke Nestor, son of Neleus, and sat back down in his place, having told his son the way to win.

The fifth to prepare his flowing-maned horses was Meriones.

Then they mounted their chariots and tossed in their lots. Achilles shook them, and the first to fall out was that of Antilochos, son of Nestor, and after him strong Eumelos drew the next place, and next was Menelaos, son of Atreus. Meriones drew the next lane to drive, and last of all the best of them all, Diomedes, drew the lane to drive his horses. Standing in line, Achilles showed them the *terma,* far away on the level plain. Next to the goal he set godlike Phoinix, squire of his father, to remember the running and certify it.

Then all held their whips high above their horses, and together flicked with their reins, and bellowed out for speed. Quickly they spread out over the plain and left the ships behind. The swirling dust clung beneath the chests of the horses like clouds of a whirlwind; their manes streamed out in the wind's current; the chariots plunged down to the ground and, again, shot up like meteors. The drivers rocked in their chariots, and the heart of each beat high with the hope of victory; they shouted to their horses, and they flew over the plain in a cloud of dust.

But when the fleet horses turned back toward the shore, then the *arete* of each began to show, and at once the field of horses was stretched out. Quickly the swift-footed horses of Eumelos went in front, and after them the stallions of Diomedes, not far behind and seemingly always about to climb into the chariot of Eumelos with their breath hot on his back and broad shoulders. And Diomedes might have passed, or at least drawn even, had not Apollo been angry with him, and dashed the whip from his hands. The tears of rage started from his eyes which watched the mares of Eumelos running ever better while his own horses slackened without the goad. But Apollo's cheating of Diomedes did not escape Athena; quickly she swept to him and returned his whip, and inspired his horses with strength. Then she descended in wrath upon Eumelos and broke the yoke of his horses. They ran off the road, the pole dragging on the ground, and he was catapulted out of the chariot over the wheel, ripping his elbows and mouth and skin, and smashing his forehead so that the tears flowed but his voice would not. Then Diomedes rushed past him, and led the field by far, for Athena had inspired strength in his horses and glory in him.

After him came fair-haired Menelaos, but Antilochos cried out to his father's horses:

"Step it up, you two! Pull as fast as you can! I'm not telling you to catch those horses of Diomedes—Athena has now inspired strength in them and glory in him—but beat the horses of Menelaos! Don't be left behind! Faster! For shame to let his mares beat you stallions! Why are you falling behind, my brave boys? Do you know what's going to happen? You'll get no more care from Nestor; he'll cut you up for dog food, if we carry off the lesser prize because you didn't try. Get going! As fast as you can! I know what I'll do, I'll slip past him where the road gets narrow. He won't get away from me!"

So he spoke, and they were terrified by their master's shouts and ran harder for a little while, and then Antilochos saw the narrow spot in the road. There was a gulley where the winter rain had run from the road creating a large pothole, and into this he forced Menelaos who shrank from a collision, but Antilochos turned his horses off the road and drove along for a bit on the shoulder. Menelaos was frightened and called out to Antilochos:

"Antilochos, that is reckless driving! Hold your horses! The road is too narrow here, but it will soon be wide enough for passing. Don't crash up your chariot and wreck the both of us!"

So he spoke, but Antilochos drove all the harder and lashed his horses for greater speed, as if he had not heard him. They ran even for about the length of a boy's diskos throw, but then the mares of Menelaos fell back, for he let up lest the horses crash, the chariots overturn, and they in their struggle for victory end up in the dust. But fair-haired Menelaos called out in anger:

"Antilochos, you are the most wretched of men! Damn you! We Achaians were wrong to say you had good sense! But you won't get the prize without swearing that you played fair!"

So he spoke, and then shouted out to his horses:

"Don't slacken up, don't stop, even though your hearts are heavy! Their feet and knees will tire before yours! Their youth is gone."

So he spoke, and they were terrified by their master's shouts and ran harder and soon caught up with the others.

Meanwhile, the Argives sitting in their assembly were watching for the horses which flew through the dust of the plain. Idomeneus, lord of the Cretans, was first to make out the horses, for he sat apart from the others, and higher up where he had a panoramic view. He heard and recognized the shouting of Diomedes, and made out his conspicuous horse, leading the others, all red except for a white mark like a full moon on his forehead. Idomeneus stood up and called to the Argives:

"Friends, am I the only one who sees the horses, or do you see them too? It seems to me that other horses are leading, another charioteer ahead. The mares of Eumelos must have come to grief on the plain, for I saw them running in front around the *terma*, but now they are nowhere to be seen and I have looked over the whole Trojan plain. Perhaps the reins slipped away from the charioteer and he could not hold them around the *terma*, and did not make the turn. I think that he must have been thrown out there and his chariot wrecked, and his mares bolted away wildly. But do get up and see for yourselves, for I cannot make it out clearly. I think that strong Diomedes is in the lead."

And swift Ajax, son of Oileus, spoke shamefully to him:

"Idomeneus, can't you hold your wind? The horses are still far out on the plain. You are not the youngest of us, and your eyes are no better than ours, but you must always blow on and on. There is no need for your wind since there are others here better than you. Those are the same mares in front as before, and the same Eumelos who holds the reins behind them."

Then the lord of the Cretans angrily answered him to his face:

"Ajax, although you are the best in abuse and stupidity, you are the worst of the Argives with that donkey's brain of yours. Now put your money where your mouth is and bet me a tripod-cauldron. We'll have Agamemnon, son of Atreus, hold the bet so that you will pay up when you find out which horses are in front."

So he spoke, and swift Ajax jumped up again in anger to retort, and the quarrel would have gone on had Achilles not risen and said to them:

"Ajax and Idomeneus, be quiet. This is not becoming, and if others were acting like you, you yourselves would be angry with them. Sit down with the others and watch for the horses. They are into the stretch and will be here soon, and then you can see for yourselves which are first and which are second."

While he spoke, Diomedes had come driving hard upon them, lashing his horses. They still ran with feet high and light, and dust still splashed at the charioteer, and the chariot plated in tin and gold still rolled hard behind the flying feet of the horses. So quickly they flew that the wheels scarcely left a trace in the soft dust. Diomedes stopped them in the middle of the crowd with the sweat dripping densely to the ground from their necks and chests. He vaulted from his shining chariot to the ground, leaned his whip against the yoke, and did not delay to take his prize, the woman and the tripod with ears which he gave to his comrades to take away, and unyoked his horses.

Next in was Antilochos who had passed Menelaos by trick rather than by speed. But even so Menelaos held his swift horses near behind and would have won clearly had the course been longer. Then came Meriones, noble squire of Idomeneus, a full spear cast behind Menelaos. His horses were beautiful but slow, and he the least talented at chariot racing. Last and behind all the others came Eumelos, dragging his lovely chariot and driving his horses before him. Seeing him, Achilles took pity and stood up among the Argives and spoke out:

"The best man has come in last, but let's give him a prize as he deserves: the second prize. The first should go to Diomedes."

So he spoke, and all agreed, and he would have given the horse to Eumelos had not Antilochos stood up to argue:

"Achilles, I shall be very angry with you if you do as you suggest. You mean to take my prize away from me thinking that, even though he is a wretched driver he is a good man. Well, he ought to have prayed to the gods, and then he would not have been last. If he is so dear to you and such a good friend, then there is plenty of gold in your tent, and bronze and sheep, and women and horses. From those give him a prize, even better than mine, and the Achaians will applaud you, but I will not give up the mare, and if anyone wants her he will have to fight me to get her."

So he spoke, but Achilles was delighted with his good friend and smiled and answered him:

"Antilochos, if you would have me bring out something special to give to Eumelos, then I will do so for your sake. I will give him a bronze corselet with a tin overlay. It will be worth something to him."

He spoke and told Automedon, his beloved companion, to bring it out of his tent. This was done, and he placed it in Eumelos' hands, and he accepted it joyfully. But then Menelaos, with heart full of bitterness and anger against Antilochos, stood up, and the herald put the staff in his hands and called for silence among the Argives, and he proceeded to speak:

"Antilochos, you used to play fair, but what you have done now? You have besmirched my *arete*, you fouled my horses by throwing your own in front of them, even though yours are far inferior. Come now, Argives, leaders and rulers of men, judge between us, with no prejudice, so that no man can say: 'Menelaos used lies and force against Antilochos and went off with the mare Antilochos had won, for Menelaos' horses were inferior, but he has greater power and prestige.' Or rather I will judge for myself, and no man will question the decision, for it will be fair. Come here, Zeus-nurtured Antilochos, and do what is right. Stand in front of your horses and chariot, take in your hand the whip with which you drove them before, take hold of your horses and swear by Poseidon the Earthholder and Earthshaker that you did not foul up my chariot with a dirty trick."

Then Antilochos, once more the sportsman, answered him:

"Enough now. I am much younger than you, lord Menelaos, and you are my elder and better. You know how greedy transgressions sprout up in a young man, for his mind races on, but his judgement is lightweight. Please be patient with me. I will give to you the mare which I won. If you demand something of my own besides, I would give it to you, Zeus-nurtured, rather than have fallen for all time from your favor and be wrong in the eyes of heaven."

He spoke, and led up the mare and gave her to Menelaos whose anger softened. He said:

"Antilochos, although I was angry I will now give way to you, since you were not flighty or lightheaded before now. Your youth got the better of your brain. You will not play tricks on your betters another time. Another man might not have won me over, but you have suffered much and worked hard for my sake, as have your noble father and you brother. Therefore, I shall be swayed by your supplication, and I will even give you the mare, although she is mine, so that all may see and know that my heart is never arrogant and stubborn."

He spoke, and gave the mare to a comrade of Antilochos to lead away, and took for himself the glittering cauldron. Fourth, in the order he had driven, Meriones took the two talents of gold. But the fifth prize, the two-handled bowl, was left over. Achilles carried it through the assembly, gave it to Nestor, and stood by him and said:

"Let this now be yours, venerable sir, to keep in memory of the burial of Patroklos, since never again will you see him among the Argives. I simply want to give you this prize, since never again will you fight with your fists, nor wrestle, nor compete in the javelin, nor in the footraces, for already the difficulties of old age are upon you."

So speaking, he placed it in Nestor's hands. And he received it joyfully and answered:

"You're right, my boy, everything you said is true. My joints aren't what they used to be, nor my feet, and my hands no longer shoot out lightly from my shoulders. If only I were young and strong again as I was back then when the Epeans were burying Amarynkeas in Bouprasion and his sons set up prizes in honor of the king. There wasn't a man like me then, not a one. I beat Klytomedeas, son of Enops, in the boxing. In the wrestling, only Ankaios of Pleuron stood up to me, and I beat him too. Iphiklos was fast, but I beat him in the races, and I beat both Phyleas and Polydoros in the javelin. I only lost in the horse race because the Aktorians—they were Siamese twins, you know—outmanned me in pursuit of the biggest prizes. One of them took the reins and did the driving while the other used the whip and talked to the horses. That's what I was like back then, but now the youngsters have to do such things. I have to bow to old age, but then I bowed to no man. Now you go along and honor your fallen comrade with these games. I accept this gladly; it does my heart good that you remember me as your faithful friend, and that you do not forget the honor which is my due among our people. May the gods grant you proper joy for this."

So he spoke, and Achilles, having listened to all these praises of Nestor, returned to the assembly of the Achaians. Next he set out the prizes for the painful boxing. He led out and tethered in the field a mule, six years old, hardworking, and unbroken, and for the loser he set out a two-handled goblet. He then stood up and spoke to the Argives:

"I invite two men, the best among you, to box for these prizes. All you Achaians bear witness that he to whom Apollo gives endurance will take away to his tent this hardworking mule. The one who is beaten will take the two-handled goblet."

He spoke, and immediately a huge and powerful man, Epeios son of Panopeus, well skilled in boxing rose up, seized the mule, and said:

"Let the one who wants the two-handled goblet come near, for I say that none of you will beat me at boxing and take the mule; I am the greatest. Isn't enough that I am deficient on the battlefield? A man can't be number one in everything. But I know what's going to happen here to any opponent of mine. I'll tear him limb-from-limb and smash his bones together. Let his friends huddle nearby to carry him out after my fists have beaten him to a pulp."

So he spoke, and they all kept their mouths shut. At last one
Euryalos stood up. Diomedes was his second, and encouraged him,
and wanted the victory for him. First he pulled the boxing belt on
around his waist, and then gave him the *himantes* carefully cut from
the hide of an ox. The two men, belted up, stepped into the middle of
the assembly, squared off, and put up their hands. Then they fell
upon each other with their heavy hands mixing it up. There was a
gnashing of teeth, and sweat poured off their limbs. Then Epeios
rushed in and hit him on the jaw as he peered through his guard,
and his knees buckled. As in the water rippled by the north wind a
fish jumps in the seaweed of the shallows and disappears again into
the dark water, so Euryalos left the ground from the blow. But great-
hearted Epeios held him upright in his hands. Euryalos' friends
gathered around him and led him through the assembly with his feet
dragging as he spat up thick blood and rolled his head over on one
side. They led him completely dazed, and they had to return for the
two-handled goblet.

Now Achilles set out the prizes for the third contest, the painful
wrestling. For the winner there was a huge tripod to be set over the
fire. The Achaians among themselves valued it at twelve oxen. He
placed a woman, skilled in the work of her hands, for the loser, and
they rated her at four oxen. Then Achilles stood up and spoke out:

"Rise up, two who would try for this prize."

So he spoke, and up rose huge Ajax, son of Telamon, and to
oppose him the crafty Odysseus who knew every trick. The two men,
belted up, stepped into the middle of the assembly, and grabbed
each other with their heavy arms looking like rafters which a
renowned architect has fitted in the roof of a high house. Their
backs creaked under the force of violent, stubborn, tugging hands.
Wet sweat poured down, and raw places all along their ribs and
shoulders broke out bright red with blood, and they continued to
struggle for victory and the wrought tripod. Odysseus could not
bring down Ajax nor throw him, nor could Ajax throw Odysseus who
was too strong. Gradually the Achaians began to be restless, and
huge Ajax said:

"Son of Laertes, either lift me, or I will lift you. The outcome is
known to Zeus."

So speaking he lifted, but Odysseus did not forget his tricks.
Odysseus caught him with a stroke behind the knee, and threw him

over backward, so that he fell on the chest of Ajax as the crowd applauded. Next, Odysseus tried to lift Ajax, but could not raise him
clear of the ground, so he hooked his knee again but they fell
together and both were soiled with dust. Then they would have
wrestled a third time, but Achilles stood up and called to them to
stop:

"Wrestle no more now! Don't wear yourselves out and get hurt!
You are both winners. Go off and divide the prizes and let the rest of
the Achaians compete."

So he spoke, and they listened to him and obeyed, and wiped off
the dust and put on their clothes.

Now Achilles set out prizes for the foot-race: a silver mixing bowl,
a work of art, which held only six measures but surpassed all others
in its loveliness. This Achilles made the prize for the fastest runner
in memory of his comrade. For second place he set out a large
and fatted ox, and for the last place he set out half a talent of gold.
Then Achilles stood up and spoke out:

"Rise up, you who would try for this prize."

So he spoke, and there stood up swift Ajax, son of Oileus, and
crafty Odysseus, and Antilochos the son of Nestor, the best runner of
the young men. They lined up, and Achilles showed them the *terma*.
They sprinted from the *nyssa,* and soon Ajax was in front, but
Odysseus was running so close behind that his feet were hitting Ajax'
tracks before the dust could settle back into them, and his breath
was hitting the back of Ajax' neck. All the Achaians were cheering
his effort to win, shouting for him to turn it on. But when they were
in the stretch, Odysseus said a silent prayer to the gray-eyed Athena:

"Hear me, goddess, be kind to me and come with extra strength
for my feet."

So he prayed, and Pallas Athena heard him, and lightened his
limbs, feet and arms too. As they were making their final sprint for
the prize, Ajax slipped and fell (Athena tripped him) where dung
was scattered on the ground from bellowing oxen, and he got the
stuff in his mouth and up his nose. So Odysseus took away the
mixing bowl, because he finished first, and the ox went to Ajax. He
stood with his hands on the horns of the ox, spitting out dung, and
said to the Argives:

"Oh, shit! That goddess tripped me, that goddess who has always
stood by Odysseus and cared for him like a mother."

They all roared in laughter at him, and then came Antilochos to take the prize for last place, and grinned as he spoke to the Argives:

"Friends, you all know well the truth of what I say, that still the gods continue to favor the older men. Look here, Ajax is older than I, if only by a little, but Odysseus is out of another age and truly one of the ancients. But his old age is, as they say, a lusty one. I don't think any Achaian could match his speed, except Achilles."

So he spoke and glorified the swift-footed son of Peleus. And Achilles answered him:

"Antilochos, your kind words for me shall not have been said in vain, for I shall add another half talent of gold to your prize."

So speaking he placed it in his hands, and Antilochos received it joyfully. Then Achilles brought into the assembly and set out the spear and shield and helmet of Sarpedon which Patroklos had stripped from his body. Then he stood up and spoke out:

"I invite two men, the best among you, to contend for these prizes. Let them put on their armour and take up their bronze spears and stand up to each other in the trial of close combat. The fighter who is the first of the two to get in a stroke at the other's body, to get through armour and draw blood, to that man I will give this magnificent silver-studded sword. Both men will carry off the armour of Sarpedon and have it in common, and I will treat them both to a good dinner in my tent."

So he spoke, and huge Ajax son of Telamon rose up, and the son of Tydeus, strong Diomedes. When they had donned their armour, they came together in the middle, furious for combat, with fierce faces, and all the Achaians were astonished. They closed and made three charges at one another. Then Ajax stabbed at Diomedes' shield, but did not get through to the skin for the corselet held. Then Diomedes reached over the great shield and tried to hit his neck with the tip of his spear again and again. When the Achaians saw this they feared for Ajax and called for them to stop and to divide the prizes evenly. But Achilles gave to Diomedes the sword with its sheath and belt.

Next Achilles set out a lump of pig-iron, which Eetion the mighty used to hurl. But when Achilles killed him, he brought this away in his ships with the rest of the booty. Then Achilles stood up and spoke out:

"Rise up, you who would try for this prize. Whoever wins will have a supply of iron for five years, and neither his shepherd nor his ploughman will have to go to the city for iron, but will have it already at home.

So he spoke, and up stood Polypoites and Leonteus and Ajax son
of Telamon, and Epeios. They stood in a line, and Epeios took the
weight, and whirling let it fly, but the Achaians all laughed. Second
to throw was Leonteus, and third huge Ajax hurled it from his heavy
hand, and surpassed the marks of all the others. But when
Polypoites took the weight, he overthrew the entire field by as far as
an ox-herd can cast his stick, and they applauded him. The
comrades of Polypoites took the prize from the king to the hollow
ships.

Once again Achilles set out gloomy iron, this time for the archers.
He set out ten double-bladed axes, and ten with single blades. Far
away in the sands he planted the mast of a ship, and to it tethered a
tremulous wild pigeon by a thin string attached to her foot, and
challenged the archers to shoot at her:

"He who hits the wild pigeon will take home all the double axes.
He who hits the string, having missed the bird, will be the loser and
take the single axes."

So he spoke and up stood Teukros and Meriones squire of
Idomeneus. They shook their lots in a bronze helmet, and Teukros'
jumped out first. He let fly a strong shot, but did not promise a
sacrifice to Apollo, and so missed the bird, for Apollo begrudged
him that, but he did snap the string with his arrow, and the pigeon
soared swiftly up toward the sky, while the string dangled toward the
ground. The Achaians thundered approval. Meriones in a fury of
haste caught the bow from Teukros' hand, and readied his arrow,
and promised Apollo a grand sacrifice of first born lambs. High up
under the clouds he saw the wild pigeon and as she circled he struck
her in the body under the wing. The shaft passed clean through and
out of her and dropped back to stick in the ground next to his foot,
but the bird dropped onto the top of the mast. Her head drooped and
the beating wings went slack and the spirit of life fled from her and
she dropped down from the mast, and the people were astonished.
Then Meriones gathered up all ten double axes, and Teukros carried
the single axes back to his ship.

Next Achilles carried into the assembly and set out a long spear
and an untarnished cauldron with flowery designs on it, worth an ox.
And the spear-throwers stood up. The son of Atreus, king
Agamemnon rose, and so did Meriones, squire of Idomeneus. But
Achilles said to them:

"King Agamemnon, since we all know that you surpass all others
and are the best by far of spear-throwers, take the cauldron, but let

us give the spear to Meriones, if you agree."

So he spoke, and Agamemnon, the lord of men, did not disagree. Now the games broke up, and the people scattered, each to his own ship. The rest of them thought of their dinners and of sweet sleep, but Achilles alone still wept as he remembered his beloved companion. All-conquering sleep would not come to him, and he tossed from side to side in longing for Patroklos.

2 Homer, *Odyssey* 8.97-253   *ca.* 725 B.C.

Odysseus, in the tenth year of wandering in his attempt to return home to Ithaka after the fall of Troy, has been washed up on the shore of a strange land. He is treated hospitably by the native Phaeacians, who inquire nothing of him, and after a meal the bard, Demodokos, entertains them with songs of the Trojan War which evoke memories and tears from Odysseus. His host, the gracious Alcinoos, notes this, and speaks:

"Leaders and councillors of the Phaeacians, we have had enough now of feasting and of the lyre-singing which properly accompanies an abundant table. Let us instead go out and divert ourselves with various athletic contests so that when our guest goes home he will tell his friends how we surpass others in boxing and wrestling and jumping and foot-racing."

So he spoke and went out, and a crowd of thousands followed him, and many sturdy youths stood up as contestants.

The first contest was in running. They sprinted from the *nyssa,* and flew in a cloud of dust across the plain. Klytoneus won by a long way; he left the others behind by the width of a field which a team of mules can plough in a day. Next they tried the painful wrestling, and Euryalos was the best of all. Amphialos jumped the furthest, and Elatreus won easily with the diskos. In the boxing the winner was Laodamas son of Alcinoos. When all had enjoyed the contests, Laodamas said to the young men:

"Hey gang! Let's go ask the stranger if he knows any sport and can show us something. He's well built, and from the look of his thighs and calves, as well as his arms and neck, he must be strong. He's not so old either, although he does look worn-out by hardships. There's nothing like the sea for knocking the stuffing out of the strongest man."

Euryalos answered him and said:

"Okay, Laodamas, you've made your point. Now let's see you do something about it."

Hearing this, Laodamas went into the middle of the crowd and addressed Odysseus:

"Won't you too, sir, try your hand at some contest, that is, if you know any, but you have the look of an athlete to me. There is no greater fame for a man than that which he wins with his footwork or the skill of his hands. Have a try now and put away your cares. Your journey home is near at hand, and we have already prepared for you a ship and crew."

Crafty Odysseus replied to him:

"Laodamas, why do you young chaps mock me with such an invitation? My heart is more set on grief than games, for I have toiled long and suffered much. I am here in your gathering only as a suppliant to beg my passage home from your king and your people."

Then Euryalos interrupted and sneered at him:

"As I see it, stranger, you're no good at sports like a real man. You remind me of a master of peddling sailors, one who trades from port to port with thoughts for nothing but cargoes and loads and especially profits. You're no athlete."

Crafty Odysseus glared at him and thundered:

"You're no gentleman, sir! You behave like a clod! It is so true that the Gods do not give total grace, a complete endowment of both beauty and wit, to all men alike. There will be one man who is less than average in build, and yet the Gods will so crown his words with a flower of beauty that all who hear him are moved. When he holds forth in public it is with assurance, yet with so sweet a modesty that it makes him shine out above the general run of men. Another man will be as handsome as the Gods, yet will lack that strand of charm twined into his words. Take yourself, for example: a masterpiece in body which not even a god could improve, but empty in the head. Your sneering made my heart beat faster. I am no ninny at sports, as you would have it. Indeed I think I was among the best in my time, but now I exist in pain and misery, having risked and endured much in the wars of men and the toils of the sea. Yet despite the ravages of these evil things I will try your tests of strength. Your sneer has galled me and your words have stung me."

He spoke and sprang to his feet still clothed and seized a diskos which was bigger and heavier than those the Phaeacians had been hurling among themselves. Whirling, he hurled it from his mighty

hand, and the stone whistled through the air. Those Phaeacians of
the long oars, those master mariners, hit the dirt beneath the
hurtling stone which soared so freely from the hero's hand that it
overpassed the marks of every other. And Athena, now disguised as
a Phaeacian, set the *terma* and called out:

"Even a blind man, sir, could judge your throw by feeling for it; it
is not mixed in with the others, but far out in front. You may take
heart from this contest, for no Phaeacian will come close, much less
beat you."

So she spoke, and Odysseus was cheered to have found a friend in
that crowd, and with lighter heart he said to the Phaeacians:

"Now then, young sports, match this throw, and as soon as you do,
I'll throw another even longer. For the rest, let anyone whose spirit
or temper prompts him step out and take me on in boxing or
wrestling or foot-racing, or whatever. You have worked me up to
such a pitch that I shall not flinch from anything, nor refuse a bout
to any single Phaeacian, except my host Laodamas. Only a dim-
witted fool would compete with his benefactor. To challenge one's
host, while being kindly treated in a foreign land, would be to cut off
one's nose to spite one's face. But I refuse no other man, nor dodge
any competition. In no sport do I disgrace myself. I can handle well
the polished bow, and I can send my spear further than others can
shoot their arrows. I fear only that in the foot-races some of the
Phaeacians may beat me, for I have been shamefully mauled by
constant waves on a bare ship. The joints of my knees are therefore
feeble."

So he spoke, and all were hushed in silence. Then Alcinoos
answered and said:

"Sir, what you have said to us is not unwelcome for it is natural
that you should want to show your *arete* since you were angered by
that man standing up in the gathering and sneering at you as if at
your *arete*, although no man in his right senses would do so. But
come now, listen and remember the abilities which Zeus has given us
so that you can relate them to some other hero when you dine in your
own house with your wife and children. I confess that we are not
polished fighters with our fists, nor wrestlers, but we can run swiftly
and are experts on shipboard. We love eating and harp-playing and
dancing and changes of clothes and hot baths and our beds. But
come, let us have the best dancers of the Phaeacians dance before us
so that when our guest goes home he will tell his friends how we

surpass others in seamanship and running and dancing and singing."

3 Pausanias I.44.1 ca. A.D. 170

Pausanias was an avid tourist who visited Greece in the middle of the second century after Christ and who ultimately wrote a "guide book" to Greece based upon his observations and research. His descriptions of statues at Olympia make him the single most important ancient source for the names and careers of various athletes. He also frequently reveals details of athletic practices which were incidental to the monuments which he was describing. One such case is in his description of the cemetery at Megara:

Near the tomb of Koroibos is buried Orsippos who won the *stadion* at Olympia (720 B.C.). While the other athletes in the competition wore loin-cloths in accordance with the ancient practice, he ran naked ... I think that the loin-cloth slipped off deliberately at Olympia, for he recognized that a nude man can run more easily than one who is girt.

4 Thucydides I.6.5-6 ca. 420 B.C.

The Athenian historian Thucydides was an eyewitness to many of the events of the struggle between Sparta and Athens, and his account of the Peloponnesian War is usually very reliable. Here he speaks of the more general history of the Greeks and appears to contradict the evidence of both Pausanias (above, no. 3) and of archaeology. It is unfortunate that we cannot know what Thucydides had in mind by his phrase: "not many years since."

The Lacedaimonians were the first to take off their clothes and, having stripped in the open, to annoit themselves with oil during their exercises. In early times, even in the Olympic Games, the athletes competed with loin-cloths around their genitals, and it is not many years since that custom has stopped. Even still today those barbarians, especially in Asia, who have contests in boxing and wrestling, compete wearing loin-cloths. Indeed, one could show that the Greeks of old practiced many customs like those of today's barbarians.

5   Philostratos *On Gymnastics* 32-33   *ca.* A.D. 230
Although many handbooks on physical training were available in
antiquity, only one has survived. Although later in date than the
period in which we are most interested, Philostratos' manual still
contains much information of interest, and it often reflects earlier
practices. We will examine many passages from this manual which
relate to the different competitive events.

The best candidate for the *dolichos* should have a powerful neck
and shoulders like the candidate for the *pentathlon,* but he should
have light, slender legs like the runners in the *stadion.* The latter stir
their legs into the sprint by using their hands as if they were wings.
The runners in the *dolichos* do this near the end of the race, but the
rest of the time they move almost as if they were walking, holding up
their hands in front of them, and because of this they need stronger
shoulders.

No one any longer makes any distinction between the physiques of
the contestants for the *hoplitodromos,* the *stadion,* and the *diaulos*
since Leonidas of Rhodes (164-152 B.C.) won all three races in four
successive Olympiads. Still, we should distinguish between those
entering just one of these races and those who enter all of them. The
entrant in the *hoplitodromos* should have a long waist, a
well-developed shoulder, and a knee tilted upward in order that,
with these parts supporting it, the shield may be carried easily. Of
the runners in the *stadion,* which is the least strenuous of the sports,
those of symmetrical build are very good, but better than these are
those who are not too tall but yet a bit too tall for their proportion.
Excessive height, however, lacks firmness, like a plant which has
shot up too high. They should be solidly built, for the fundamental
thing in running well is to stand well. Their proportions should be as
follows: the legs should balance with the shoulders, the chest should
be smaller than normal and should contain sound inner organs, the
knee must be limber, the shank straight, the hand above average
size, the muscles should be only medium, for oversize muscles are
fetters to speed. Candidates for the *diaulos* should be stronger than
those for the *stadion,* but lighter than those in the *hoplitodromos.*
Those who compete in all three races should be put together from
the best and should possess a combination of all the qualifications
which are needed in each single race. Do not think that this is
impossible, for there have been such runners even in our own day.

6   Herodotus VI.105-106   490 B.C.

Herodotus, who wrote in about 430 B.C. and frequently relied upon the accounts of eye-witnesses describes here a part of the preparations of the Athenians to meet the Persians on the plain of Marathon. In particular, we are concerned with the courier sent to Sparta to appeal for help. It should be noted that we do not know his name for certain; he is called Philippides in some manuscripts, Pheidippides in others.

Before leaving for Marathon and while they were still in Athens, the generals sent a messenger to Sparta, one Philippides, an Athenian who was also a *hemerodromos* who was used to doing this sort of thing. According to him, as he reported to the Athenians later, Pan appeared to him on Mt. Parthenion above Tegea. Pan called out his name and ordered Philippides to ask the Athenians why they paid no honors to him, even though he was well-intentioned toward them, and had been helpful to them many times in the past, and would be so again in the future. The Athenians believed that this story was true and, when their affairs were settled once more, they established a shrine of Pan at the foot of the Acropolis, and they have appeased him from the time of his message with annual sacrifices and a torch-race. This Philippides, who had been sent by the generals then when he said that Pan appeared to him, arrived in Sparta on the day after he left Athens.

7   Philostratos, *On Gymnastics* 35   ca. A.D. 230

Let us turn to the wrestlers. The proper wrestler should be rather taller than one who is precisely proportioned, but formed like those who are precisely proportioned with a neck which is neither long, nor set down into the shoulders. The latter is, to be sure, suitable, but it looks more deformed than athletic, just as among the statues of Herakles, the more pleasing and godlike are those which are noble and without short necks. The neck should, then, be upright like that of a horse which is beautiful and knows it, and the throat should come down to the collarbone on either side. The shoulders should be drawn together and the tops of the shoulders should stand up straight; this contributes size to the wrestler and a noble appearance and strength and a greater wrestling ability. Such shoulders are good guards when the neck is bent and twisted by wrestling, for they give the head a firm base which extends all the way from the arms. A well-marked arm is good for wrestling. What I call a well-marked arm is the following: broad veins begin from the neck, one on each side of the throat, and travel across the shoulders to descend into the hands, and are prominent on the upper arms and forearms. Those who have these veins close to the surface and more visible than usual derive no strength from them, and the veins themselves look ugly like varicose veins. Those who have veins which are deep and slightly swelling appear to have a delicate and distinct spirit in their arms. Such veins make the arms of an aging man grow younger, while in a young man they reveal potential and promise in wrestling.

The better chest is prominent and protruding, for the organs are situated in it as if in a stout and well-shaped room, and the organs are excellent, strong, healthy, and showing spirit at the appropriate time. But the moderately protruding chest is also beautiful, if it has been hardened with ridges all around, for it is strong and vigourous and, even though it is not the best for wrestling, it is better than the other kinds of chest. I hold that hollow sunken chests ought not to be seen, much less be exercised, for they suffer from stomach cramps, poor organs, and short wind. The lower abdomen should be drawn in—this is a useless burden to the wrestler—and it should rest upon thighs which are not hollow, but well rounded. Such thighs press together and are adequate for everything in wrestling, and pressed together they give pain rather than receive it.

The straight back is beautiful, but the slightly curved is more athletic since it is better adapted to the bent and forward-leaning posture of wrestling. The back should not be distinguished by a hollow backbone, for this will be lacking in marrow and the vertebrae can be twisted and compressed by wrestling, and can even slip inward; but this is my opinion rather than established fact. The hip joint, since it serves as the pivot for the parts of the body both above and below it, must be supple, well turned and easy to rotate. This is affected by the length of the hip and by its extraordinary fleshiness. The part of the leg under the hip should not be either too smooth or too fleshy, for the former is a sign of weakness, the latter of a lack of exercise. Rather, it should protrude markedly and in a way suitable for a wrestler.

Sides which are flexible and which also lift up the chest are adequate for both offensive and defensive wrestling. Men with such sides who are beneath their opponents are difficult to subdue, and they are no easy burden when on top of their opponents. Narrow buttocks are weak, fat ones slow, but well formed buttocks are an asset for everything. A solid thigh turned outwards combines strength with beauty, and it gives good support which is even better if the lower legs are not bowed, for the thigh then rests upon a straight knee. Ankles which are not straight but slant inward over-throw the whole body just as crooked bases tip columns over.

8   Pausanias VI.4.2   *ca.* A.D. 170
Pausanias is now at Olympia as he is for nearly all of books V and VI.

   There is a statue of a Sikyonian man, a pankratiast, named Sostratos. His nickname was Akrochersites [Fingerman], because he would grab his opponent by the fingers and bend them and not let go until his opponent surrendered. He won twelve victories at Isthmia and Nemea combined, three at Olympia, and two at Delphi. The 104th Olympiad [364 B.C.] at which Sostratos won his first victory is not accredited by the Eleans, because the games were not held by them, but by the Pisans and the Arkadians. Next to the statue of Sostratos is one of a wrestler in the men's category, Leontiskos from Messene on the Sicilian straits. He was crowned once at Delphi and twice at Olympia. It is said that his wrestling style was similar to that used by Sostratos in the *pankration;* that is, he did not know how to throw his opponents and thus beat them by bending their fingers.

9   Lucian, *Anacharsis* 1-8 and 28-29   [*ca.* 590 B.C.]
Lucian, who was active around the middle of the second century after Christ, wrote a number of essays. This one is set in Athens and purports to be a conversation between Solon, the Athenian lawgiver, and the Skythian Anacharsis who had come to Greece from his home on the Black Sea in quest of wisdom. Lucian appears to want us to understand Solon as the representative of civilization and Anacharsis as the representative of naive barbarism, and he seems to have picked athletics for the topic of their "conversation" as that aspect of Greek civilization which would be the strangest to the foreigner. It is not completely clear who "wins" the debate, nor exactly where Lucian's own sympathies lie; perhaps the ambiguity is

deliberate. The athletic details which we learn from Lucian are sometimes vague or even anachronistic for the supposed date of the confrontation between Solon and Anacharsis, but Lucian does give us a general impression which is correct, a vivid image of the role of athletics in everyday Greek civic life.

ANACHARSIS: Solon, what are your young men doing? Some of them are all wrapped up together but trying to trip each other; others are strangling and tackling one another, and grovelling in the mud, wallowing around like pigs. But in the beginning, as I saw for myself, as soon as they took off their clothes they oiled themselves and took turns rubbing each other down quite peacefully. But I don't understand what has happened to them, for now they push and tug at one another and butt their foreheads together like rams. Now look there! That man picked up the other man by the legs and threw him to the ground, and then fell on top of him and will not let him up, but keeps pushing him into the mud. Now he has got his legs wrapped around the other man's mid-section and he is grabbing his throat with his forearm and strangling him, and the other one is slapping the first on the shoulder in order to signal, I guess, that he has had enough and doesn't want, poor fellow, to be choked completely. Not even on account of the expensive oil do they avoid getting dirty. Instead they rub off the ointment, and pile on the mud mixed with buckets of sweat and make themselves ridiculous, at least to me, as they slip from each other's hands like eels.

In the open part of the courtyard others are doing exactly the same thing, though not in the mud. Rather, they have put down a thick layer of sand in a trench and they sprinkle one another voluntarily, piling the dust on like roosters, so that (I guess) it will be difficult to escape from the holds since the sand removes the slipperiness and gives a better grip on a dry surface.

Others, upright and covered with dust, are hitting and kicking each other. This one looks like he is going to spit out his teeth, poor fellow, with his mouth so full of blood and sand. As you see, he got a belt on the jaw. And the official—I take him to be one of the officials from his purple cloak—does not separate them and stop the fight; rather, he incites them and cheers the man who landed the punch.

Over there others are all in a lather, bobbing up and down as if they were running, but never moving from their places. Now they are jumping up and kicking the air.

Please tell me what good is being accomplished by all this.

Frankly, it looks to me more like insanity than anything else, and you are not going to convince me easily that men who act like that don't belong in the looney bin.

SOLON: Of course they look that way to you, Anacharsis, because what they are doing is strange to you and very different from the customs of your native Skythia. There is probably much in your education and exercises which would seem strange to us Greeks if one of us happened to look in upon it as you are doing now. But take heart, my good man, it is not insanity, nor even for the sake of wanton violence that they beat one another and wallow in the mud and throw dust over each other. What they are doing has some usefulness and is not without pleasure, and it strengthens their bodies to a great extent. As a matter of fact, if you stay for a time in Greece, as I hope you will, before long you will belong to the muddy or the dusty club. You will find out that what they are doing is very pleasant as well as useful.

ANACHARSIS: Thank you very much, Solon, but you Greeks can keep such pleasures for yourselves. If anyone tries to treat me to such pleasures he will find out why we carry daggers in our belts! But tell me anyway, what do you call these things? Are there words to describe what they are doing?

SOLON: We call the place a *gymnasion,* Anacharsis, and it is sacred to Lykeian Apollo. You see his statue over there, the one in the pose of leaning against a pillar with a bow in his left hand. His right hand, bent back over his head as if from the fatigue of long exertion, shows that the god is resting. What is going on is called athletics in general. The specific name for what is happening in the mud as well as in the dust is wrestling. Those who are standing upright and punching one another are practicing what we call the *pankration,* and we have other types of athletics too—boxing, the diskos, jumping, etc. For all of these we hold contests and the winner in each is the one who is the best, and he gets prizes.

(28-29) SOLON: The mud and the dust, which seemed so ridiculous to you in the beginning, are put down for the following reasons. First, so that they may fall safely on a soft surface rather than a hard one. Next, they are necessarily slipperier when they are coated with sweat and mud. Although you compared this to eels, it is neither useless nor ridiculous; it makes a considerable contribution to strength when they are slippery and one tries to hold on while the other tries to slip away. And don't think that it is easy to pick up a man who is sweaty and muddy and has oil on as well. As I said earlier, all this is useful in war in the event that one has to pick up a wounded comrade and carry him out of the fight, or grab an enemy and bring him back to one's own lines. For such reasons we train them to the limits and set the most difficult tasks so that they can do the lesser ones with greater ease.

We believe that the dust is useful for the opposite purpose, to prevent a man from slipping away once caught. Once they have been trained with the mud to hold on to what would get away because of its oiliness, they are taught to escape from the opponent's hands when they are caught in a firm grip. In addition, the dust is thought to stop profuse sweating, to prolong strength, and to prevent harm to their bodies from the wind blowing on them when their pores are open. Finally, the dust rubs off the filth and makes the man cleaner. I would like to take one of those white-skinned fellows who live in the shade and put him next to any athlete you might pick out of the Lykeion (after I had washed off the mud and dust), and then find out which you would rather resemble. I know that you would choose immediately, without even waiting to see what each could do, to be firm and hard rather than soft and like a marshmallow with thin blood withdrawing to the interior of the body.

10   Philostratos, *On Gymnastics* 9-10 and 34   *ca* A.D. 230

Boxing was a discovery of the Lacedaimonians, and Polydeukes was the best at it and for this reason the poets sang of him in this event [see below, no. 11]. The ancient Lacedaimonians boxed for the following reason: they had no helmets, nor did they think it proper to their native land to fight in helmets. They felt that a shield, properly used, could serve in the place of a helmet. Therefore they practiced boxing in order to know how to ward off blows to the face, and they hardened their faces in order to be able to endure the blows which landed. After a time, however, they quit boxing and the *pankration* as well, because these contests ae decided by one opponent acknowledging defeat and this might give an excuse for her detractors to accuse Sparta of a lack of spirit.

The ancient boxing equipment was the following: the four fingers were bound up so that they extended beyond the strap sufficiently to allow the boxer to clench his fist. The strap continued to the forearm as a support for the wrist. Now the equipment has changed. They tan the hide of a fat ox and work it into the boxing *himas* which is sharp and protrudes from the hand, and the thumb is not bound up with the fingers in order to prevent additional wounds, and thus the whole hand does not fight. For this reason they also prohibit pigskin *himantes* in the stadium because they believe them to cause painful and slow-healing wounds.

[34] The boxer should have a long hand and strong forearms and upper arms, broad shoulders and a long neck. Thick wrists strike harder blows, thinner ones are flexible and strike more easily. He should have solid hips for support, since the thrust of striking out will unbalance him if his body is not set upon firm hips. I regard fat calves as worthless in every sport, and especially boxing. They are too slow for both offensive and defensive footwork. He should have a straight calf of proper proportion to his thigh, and his thighs should be set well apart from each other. The shape of the boxer is better for offense if his thighs do not come together. The best boxer has a small belly, for he is nimble and has good wind. On the other hand, a big belly will give some advantage to a boxer, for it will get in the way of the opponent who is striking for the face.

11   Theocritus, *Idylls* 22.27-135   *ca.* 275 B.C.
The Hellenistic poet Theocritus here gives us his version of an episode in the myth of Jason's quest for the Golden Fleece in his ship Argo.

Now the Argo had escaped the Clashing Rocks and the baneful mouth of snowy Pontus [the Bosphorus] and had come to the land of the Bebrykians, bearing the dear sons of the gods. There the heroes converged from both sides of the ship, descended the gangplank, and left Jason's ship. They stepped off onto a deeply sanded shore of a headland protected from the wind and busied themselves with speading their bedrolls and gathering firewood. But Castor and Polydeukes went off by themselves straying apart from their comrades and marvelling at the many varieties of trees growing wild on the mountain. Beneath a smooth cliff they found an everflowing spring, filled to the brim with pure water; the pebbles below flashed like crystal or silver from the depths. Lofty pines grew nearby, poplars, plane-trees, tapering cypresses, and there were also fragrant flowers, work for fuzzy bees. A gigantic man was sitting there and sunning himself, an awesome sight. His ears were crushed from the rigors of boxing, his mighty chest and his broad back bulged with flesh of iron; he was like a colossal statue of hammered metal. The muscles on his firm arms just below the shoulder stood out like rounded stones which a winter's torrent rolls and polishes in great swirling eddies. Over his back there was slung a lion's skin fastened at his neck by the paws. And Polydeukes spoke to him thus:

POLYDEUKES: Good day, stranger, whoever you are. What people are they who own this land?

AMYKOS: Good day? How can the day be good when it brings to me men I never saw before?

POLYDEUKES: Do not be afraid. We are not evil men, nor were our fathers before us.

AMYKOS: I'm not afraid, and I'm not likely to learn to be afraid from the likes of you.

POLYDEUKES: Are you completely uncultured, always perverse and sneering?

AMYKOS: I am what you see, and I'm not trespassing on your land.

POLYDEUKES: Oh, well, come along with us and you will return home again with gifts of friendship.

AMYKOS: I don't want any gifts, and I've got none for you.

POLYDEUKES: Well, may we at least have a drink of this water?

AMYKOS: You'll find out when you're a lot thirstier than now.

POLYDEUKES: If you want money just say how much.

AMYKOS: I want you to put up your dukes and fight me like a man.

POLYDEUKES: In boxing? Or may we kick each other's legs too, and . . . .

AMYKOS: Shut up, put'em up, and do your damnedest.

POLYDEUKES: Wait! Is there a prize for which we will fight?

AMYKOS: If you win, you beat me, and if I win, I beat you.

POLYDEUKES: Gamecocks fight on such terms.

AMYKOS: I don't give a damn if we look like gamecocks or lions. You wanted a prize, and that's it.

So spoke Amykos and he picked up and blew upon a hollow shell at whose blast the Bebrykians. whose hair is never cut, swiftly gathered beneath the shady plane-trees. And Castor, that mighty fighter, went and called the heroes from the Argo.

When the two combatants had strengthened their hands with oxhide straps and had wound the long *himantes* around their arms, they met in the middle of the gathering and breathed out mutual slaughter. At this point there was jostling between them in their eagerness to see who would get the sunlight at his back. By quick skill Polydeukes slipped by the huge man and the sun's ray struck Amykos full in the face. Then Amykos, enraged, rushed forward aiming his fist straight at the mark, but Polydeukes sidestepped and struck him on the point of his chin. Then, even more aroused, the giant battled wildly and hunching over he rushed heavily upon Polydeukes. The Bebrykians roared applause, while the heroes on the other side shouted words of encouragement to Polydeukes, for they feared that the giant fighter would press him into a corner and finish him. But Polydeukes, shifting his ground this way and that, striking now with his right, now with his left, cut Amykos up and checked his attack in spite of his huge size. The giant came to a standstill drunk with blows, and spat out red blood while all the heroes cheered when they saw the gashes around his mouth and jaws, and as his face swelled his eyes became narrower and narrower. Then Polydeukes continued to bewilder him by making feints from all directions, but when he saw that Amykos was utterly helpless, he drove his fist against his brow smack above the nose and laid bare his forehead to the bone, and Amykos went down hard, stretched out on the layers of leaves.

But he got up again, and the fight became truly bitter; they dealt each other deadly blows from the hard *himantes*. But the giant kept throwing his punches at his opponent's chest and just below his neck while Polydeukes kept on battering Amykos' face all over. The giant's flesh shrank as he sweated and from a huge man he was fast becoming a small one whereas Polydeukes displayed ever stouter limbs and a healthier color.

Then Amykos, hoping desperately for a knockout punch, seized Polydeukes' left hand in his own left hand, and leaned sideways in his forward lunge, and reached down to his right side to bring up a huge haymaker. Had he landed the blow, he would have knocked out the Spartan prince, but Polydeukes ducked out of the way and at the same time he hit Amykos beneath the left temple with a crisp right hand delivered straight from the shoulder; and blood spurted forth from Amykos' gaping temple. Immediately, with his now free left hand, he planted a punch on the giant's mouth, and the teeth rattled loose. With blows that thudded ever sharper and sharper, he battered the man's face until his cheeks were crushed in. Then finally Amykos went down flat on the ground and, dazed, he raised his hand and gave up the fight since he was close to death. But Polydeukes, though he had won, did nothing brutal to Amykos, but did make him swear never again to insult strangers.

12   Plato, *Laws* 830a-c   *ca.* 350 B.C.
In describing his ideal political constitution, Plato insists that practice in military exercises is necessary in peacetime. As a part of his argument, he uses the following analogy:
   If we were in charge of boxers or pankratiasts or competitors in similar athletics, would we send them straight into the contest without any prior training or practice? If we were boxers, for example, we would be spending the days before the bout in learning how to fight, and training and practicing all the methods which we intended to use on the day of the real fight, and imitating the real thing as far as possible. Thus, we would wear the *sphairai* instead of the *himantes,* in order to get the best possible practice in punching and counterpunching. If we happened to be short of sparring partners, do you think that the laughter of fools would stop us from hanging up a lifeless effigy and practicing on it? Even if we were in a desert and had neither live nor lifeless sparring partners, would we not resort to a very literal shadow-boxing, practicing on ourselves as it were?

13   Pausanias VIII.40.1-5   *ca.* A.D. 170
   In the *agora* of Phigaleia there is a statue of Arrhachion the pankratiast which is of the archaic style, especially in its form; the feet are not separated and the hands hang down along the sides to the hips. The statue is made of stone, and they say that there was an epigram written on the stone. This has vanished over the years, but Arrhachion won two Olympic victories before the festival of the 54th Olympiad [564 B.C.]. At this latter festival, he won a third time, partly due to the fairness of the *Hellanodikai,* and partly because of his own *arete.* As he was fighting with the last remaining of his opponents for the olive, his opponent, whoever he was, got a grip first and held Arrhachion with his legs squeezed around

Arrhachion's midsection and his hands squeezing around his neck at the same time. Meanwhile, Arrhachion dislocated a toe on his opponent's foot but was strangled and expired. At the same instant, however, Arrhachion's opponent gave up because of the pain in this toe. The Eleans proclaimed Arrhachion the victor and crowned his corpse.

There is a similar story which I know about the Argives in the case of Kreugas, a boxer from Epidamnos. The Argives gave the crown of victory at the Nemean Games to Kreugas although he was dead, because his opponent, Damoxenos of Syracuse, broke the agreement which had been reached between them. While they were boxing evening came on and they agreed in front of witnesses that each would allow the other in turn to land a punch. Now at that time boxers did not yet wear the sharp *himas* on the wrist of each hand, but boxed with the soft *himantes* which were bound in the hollow of the hand so that the fingers were left bare. These soft *himantes* were thin oxhide thongs plaited together in some ancient way. Now Kreugas aimed his punch at Damoxenos' head. Then Damoxenos told Kreugas to lift his arm and, when Kreugas had done so, Damoxenos struck him under the ribs with his fingers straight out. The combination of his sharp fingernails and the force of his blow drove his hand into Kreugas' guts. He grabbed Kreugas' intestines and tore them out and Kreugas died on the spot. The Argives expelled Damoxenos on the grounds that he had broken his agreement by giving his opponent several blows [i.e. one for each of his fingers] instead of the agreed upon one blow. They gave the victory to the dead Kreugas and erected a statue of him in Argos.

14 Philostratos, *Pictures in a Gallery* II.6   *ca.* A.D. 240
This Philostratos is probably the son-in-law of the author with the same name who wrote the treatise on gymnastics (above, nos. 5 and 7, below no. 15). He was a sophist and rhetorician who chose a description of a series of paintings as a device to exhibit his knowledge and, occasionally, to present a moral. We are to imagine him in a gallery describing the paintings to a young student-companion.

Now you have come to the Olympic Games and to the best of the contests at Olympia. This is the pankration for men. Arrhachion is being crowned although he died at the moment of his victory, and the *Hellanodikes* is crowning him. The natural contours of the land form the stadium in a simple, but ample, glen, and the Alpheios river flows by—it is a light stream, you know, and that is why it alone of all rivers flows on top of the sea—and around it grow olive trees with gray-green leaves curling like parsley.

This is part of the painting over behind the stadium we will examine presently, and many other details too, but let us now inquire into Arrhachion's deed before it is over. He seems to have overpowered not only his opponent, but the Greeks in the audience as well. They are jumping up from their seats and shouting, some waving their hands, some leaping from the ground, and others are slapping one another on the back. His astonishing feat has left the spectators beside themselves. Who is so stolid as not to shriek aloud at this athlete? This present accomplishment surpasses his already great record of two previous victories at Olympia, for this one has cost his life and he departs for the land of the blessed with the dust still on him. But do not think that this is accidental, for he planned his victory very cleverly.

And what about the wrestling: The pankratiasts, my boy, practice a dangerous brand of wrestling. They have to endure black eyes which are not safe for the wrestler, and learn holds by which one who has fallen can still win, and they must be skillful in various ways of strangulation. They bend ankles and twist arms and throw punches and jump on their opponents. All such practices are permitted in the pankration except for biting and gouging. Indeed, the Lacedaimonians permit even this, I suppose because they are training for battle, but the Elean Games prohibit biting and gouging although they do allow strangling. For this reason Arrhachion's opponent, having already a grip around his waist, thought to kill him and put an arm around his neck to choke off his breath. At the same time he slipped his legs through Arrhachion's groin and wound his feet inside Arrhachion's knees, and pulled back until the sleep of death began to creep over Arrhachion's senses. But Arrhachion was not done yet, for as his opponent began to relax the pressure of his legs, Arrhachion kicked away his own right foot and fell heavily to the left holding his opponent at the groin and with his left knee still holding his opponent's foot firmly. So violent was the fall that the opponent's left ankle was wrenched from the socket. For Arrhachion's soul, though it leaves his body feeble, still gives him strength for is purpose.

The one who is strangling Arrhachion is painted to look like a

corpse as he signals with his hand that he is giving up. But
Arrhachion is painted as are all victors. His blood is in full flower,
and sweat still glistens, and he smiles like a living man who sees his
victory.

15   Philostratos, *On Gymnastics* 31 and 55.   *ca.* A.D. 230

The pentathlete should be heavy rather than light, and light
rather than heavy. He should be tall, well built, with good carriage,
and with musculature which is neither superfluous nor inadequate.
His legs should be long rather than strictly proportionate, and his
hips should be flexible and limber for the backward bending of
throwing the javelin and the diskos and for the *halma*. He will jump
with less pain and less likelihood of breaking something in his body
if he can land softly by letting his hips down gradually. It is
necessary that his hands and fingers be long. He will hurl the
diskos considerably better if there is a large grip for the rim of the
diskos provided in the hollow of a long-fingered hand, and he will
have less trouble in throwing the javelin if his fingers are not so short
that they barely reach the *ankyle*.

The *halter* is a discovery of the pentathletes which was invented
for use in the *halma* from which it gets its name. The rules regard
jumping as the most difficult of the competitions, and they allow the
jumper to be given advantages in rhythm by the use of the flute, and
in weight by the use of the *halter*. This is a sure guide for the hands,
and leads to a clear and firm landing on the ground. The rules show
the value of this point, for they do not allow the jump to be measured
unless the footprints are perfect. The long *halteres* provide exercise
for the shoulders and the hands; the spherical *halteres* for the
fingers as well. They should be used in all exercises, both the light
and the heavy, except for the relaxing exercises.

16   Philostratos, *Pictures in a Gallery* I.24   *ca.* A.D. 240

Read the hyacinth, for it is inscribed and says that the hyacinth
sprang from the ground in honor of a lovely lad, and that it laments
him in early spring, I suppose because it was born from him when he
died. Do not be delayed by the flower in the meadow, for it grows

from him as well, no different from the earthborn blossom. The painting says that the lad's hair is "hyacinthine" and that his blood, coming to life in the earth, colors the flower. It flows from his head where struck by the diskos. The mistake told of Apollo is terrible and scarcely creditable, but we are not here as critics of the myths and are not ready to refuse them credibility. Rather, we are simply viewers of the paintings, and thus let us examine the painting and first of all the *balbis* for the diskos.

A *balbis* has been separated off; it is small and adequate only for a single standing man, and even then it holds back only the rear and the right leg (the back is facing forward) with the weight on the left leg reduced, for it is necessary that this leg is straightened and advanced together with the right arm. The attitude of the man holding the diskos must be that he turn his head to the right and bend over so far that he can see his side, and to throw he must draw himself up and put his whole right side into the throw.

This is how Apollo has thrown the diskos, for he could not have thrown it otherwise. The diskos has struck the youth who lies on top of it. He is a Laconian youth with a straight calf which is no stranger to running, his arms are already developed and the fine lines of his bones show forth. Apollo is still standing on the *balbis* with his face averted and looking down at the ground. You might say that he is frozen there by the great consternation which has befallen him.

No gentleman is Zephyros who, because he was angry with Apollo, made the diskos strike the youth, and the scene makes the wind laugh as he jeers at Apollo from his hideaway. I think that you can see him with wings at his temples, with his delicate appearance, and with a garland about his head with every kind of flower in it. Presently he will be weaving the hyacinth in with them.

17   Aristotle, *Rhetoric* 1361b   *ca.* 360 B.C.

Each age has its own beauty. In youth, it lies in the possession of a body capable of enduring all kinds of contests, whether of the race-course or of bodily strength, while the young man is himself a pleasant delight to behold. It is for this reason that pentathletes are the most beautiful; they are naturally adapted both for exertion of the body and swiftness of foot. In the prime of life, beauty lies in being naturally adapted for the toils of war, in being both a pleasure to look at and yet awe-inspiring. In old age, beauty lies in being naturally adapted to confront unavoidable tasks and in not causing annoyance to the beholder by being devoid of the disagreeable accomplishments of old age.

Strength consists of the power of moving another man as one wants, and for this it is necessary to pull or push, to lift, squeeze, or crush. A strong man is defined as being strong by virtue of his ability to do some or all of these things.

Excellence of size is defined as being superior to most men in height, weight, and girth, but in such proportion so that the movements of the body are not slowed down by excess.

Athletic excellence in a body is defined in terms of the above: strength and size, as well as in terms of speed, for to be swift is to be strong. One who can move his legs rapidly and in long strides makes a good runner. One who can grab and grapple makes a good wrestler. One who can thrust away his opponent by a blow of the fist makes a good boxer. One who excels in both boxing and wrestling makes a good pankratiast. But he who excels in everything is fit for the pentathlon.

18   [Plato] *The Lovers* 135C-137D   [400 B.C.]

Although this dialogue has come down to us with other writings by Plato, we can be certain that he did not author this piece. We do not know the date of its composition either, but its dramatic date is obviously during Socrates' lifetime. An attempt is being made to define philosophy, and the analogy drawn between philosopher and pentathlete is interesting and perhaps revealing about an attitude toward the pentathlete. As usual, Socrates plays the Devil's advocate.

I next asked him if it was not impossible for any one person to learn equally well two crafts, not to speak of many, or even two of the principal crafts. He replied:

"Do not think, Socrates, that I would maintain that the philosopher must have the same depth of knowledge about each of the crafts as the professional working in them. I mean only such knowledge of them as may reasonably be expected of a free and educated man; that is, he should be able to follow the explanations of the craftsman more readily than the others around him. He should be able to contribute an opinion of his own which will make him seem to be the most clever and accomplished of the group which might be present at any verbal or practical display of a craft."

Then, since I was still quite unsettled about his meaning, I asked him:

"Do I understand correctly the sort of man whom you mean by the philosopher? You seem to mean someone like the pentathletes in competition with the runners or the wrestlers; the former yield, you know, to the latter in their specialities, and are their inferiors, but are superior to the run-of-the-mill athletes and beat them. It is something of this sort which you seem to suggest is the effect produced by philosophy upon those who make it their pursuit; they yield to those who are first-rate in their understanding of the crafts, but surpass the others by taking second place. In this way, the man who studies philosophy finishes second in everything. That is the sort of man whom you appear to be indicating."

"It seems to me that you are quite right, Socrates," he said, "in your concept of the philosopher's position, and in your comparison of him to the pentathlete. It is precisely his nature not to be bogged down with any business, or to work things out exactly and in detail, for to do so would mean that his excessive attention to one thing would make him deficient in the rest like a craftsman. Rather, he should have moderate contact with everything."

After this answer, I was eager to know clearly what he meant, so I asked him whether he thought of good men as useful or useless.

"I would say useful, Socrates," he replied.

"Then if useful men are good, are useless men wicked?"

He agreed that they were.

"Again, do you think that philosophers are useful men or not?"

He opined that they were not only useful, but the most useful men of all.

"Come now, let us see, if what you say is true, how these second-best men are useful to us; clearly the philosopher is second-best to any particular workman in the crafts?"

He agreed.

"Well now," I went on, "If you, or one of your close friends, were to fall sick, would you fetch the second-best man into the house in order to get well again, or would you summon a doctor?"

"For my part, I would have both," he replied.

"Please do not say 'both,' I said, "but which of the two you would prefer and would summon first."

"Of course," he replied, "anyone would prefer the doctor and summon him first."

"And again, if you were in a ship that was in rough weather, to which would you rather entrust yourself and your things, the pilot or the philosopher?"

"I would chose the pilot."

"And so it will go in everything else? So long as there is a craftsman, the philosopher will not be useful?"

"Apparently," he replied.

"So now we find that the philosopher is a useless person, assuming that we will always have craftsmen, and we have agreed that useful men are good and useless men are bad?"

He had to agree with this.

"Then what follows: Shall I ask you, or will it be too ill-mannered?"

"Ask whatever you please."

"I would like," I said, "merely to recall our agreement upon what has been stated. We agree that philosophy is honorable, and that philosophers are good; we also agree that useful men are good, and useless men wicked. But then again we agreed that philosophers, so long as we have craftsmen, are useless. Have we not agreed to all of this?"

"Yes, of course," he replied.

"Then we are also agreed, according to your definition of philosophy as having the kind of knowledge which you describe about the crafts, that philosophers are useless and wicked. But I suspect that philosophers are not really wicked, my friend, and that philosophy is not just dabbling in the crafts or spending one's life in meddlesome snooping and prying and in an accumulation of learning, but something else."

19   Xenophon, *Hellenica* VII.4.29   364 B.C.
The Arkadians have ousted the Eleans from Olympia and are celebrating the Olympic Games (cf. above, no. 8) when, much to their surprise, the Eleans march against them and into the Altis. The Games have reached the following stage when the Eleans appear:

They had already finished the horse-race, and the stadium events of the pentathlon. The competitors who had reached the wrestling were no longer in the stadium, but were wrestling in the region between the stadium and the altar.

20   *Rivista di Filologia* (1956) 55-57   First Century B.C.?

*The following inscription from the island of Rhodes is sadly frag-
mentary, but the text which does survive may provide clues about the
order of the events in the pentathlon. The parts which are enclosed
in brackets are not preserved on the stone.*

[- · · · · · · · · · · -] they are to be in charge of[- · · · · · · · · -]
[- in] turn until each five times [has thrown the diskos · · · · · -]
[first] shall jump the one who threw the diskos farthest [· · · · -]
[- · · · · -] they have   ?   the *skamma* nor the [- · · · · · · · · -]
[- · · · · · · -] of the surface of the stadium [- · · · · · · · · · -]
let it be two feet. Similarly [- · · · · · · · · · · · · · · · · · · · -]
of the *kanon* and the [- · -]
? and the one at the *te[rma* ·]
of those who are [- · -]
of the wrestler [- ·]

21   Aristophanes, *The Clouds* 1-118   423 B.C.
*The purpose of this play by Aristophanes, beyond entertainment,
was an attack upon the "education" of the Sophists. Later in the
play, Aristophanes will, unfairly, present Socrates as the prime
example of Sophists. Such a representation does not seem to have affected adversely a real admiration and respect between the two men.
Neither had any love for the Sophists who taught, once paid, the use
of the power of logic in making a bad cause appear to be the right
one. In his caricature of this Sophistical system, Aristophanes begins
with a confrontation between a father, Strepsiades (the "Twisted
One" or the "Crooked One") and his son, Pheidippides (the "Sparer
of Horses").*
STREPSIADES: O dear me, O lordy, O Zeus! How long these
nights are. Will they never pass? Will the day never come? I was
certain I heard the cock crow hours ago, but my servants still are
snoring. These are new times with strange customs. There are many
reasons for avoiding war, but the best is that one can't beat one's
own servants in wartime. Look at that son of mine, wrapped up,
snoring and sweating under five thick blankets. Oh well, I might as
well bundle up and snore along. . . . . I can't sleep at all. I am
being bitten and eaten up by ticks and bedbugs, and by bills and
race-horses, all because of this son of mine. He curls his hair and
shows off his horses and drives his chariot—even in his dreams he is
riding. But I am being ruined now that the end of the month ap-

proaches and it's time to pay the interest on my loans. Light a lamp, boy! Bring my ledger! I'll tot up my creditors and see what I owe them. "$9,600 to Pasias." Why do I owe that? Oh, for that hack with the Corinthian brand. O dear, I wish my eyes had been hacked out ......

PHEIDIPPIDES [talking in his sleep]: Philon, you cheat! Stay in your own lane!

STREPSIADES: That's it. That's what has ruined me. Even in his sleep he dreams of horses.

PHEIDIPPIDES: How many laps do the war chariots run?

STREPSIADES: Not as many as you've run your father. Now then, what debt comes down on my ears after Pasias'? "$2,400 for a racing cart and wheels to Amynias."

PHEIDIPPIDES: Give the horse a roll in the dust and take him home.

STREPSIADES: But you, my boy, have already rolled me out of house and home. Some of my creditors are taking me to court, and others swear that they will impound my property for the interest I owe them.

PHEIDIPPIDES [now awake]: Father, why do you toss and turn all night long?

STREPSIADES: There's a buggered bill-collector in my mattress.

PHEIDIPPIDES: Well, please let me get some sleep.

STREPSIADES: Okay, you go ahead and sleep. You can be sure that these debts will fall on your head some day. And may there be a curse on the head of that match-maker who aroused me to marry your mother. My life in the country was so nice, untidy, easy-going, unrestrained, brimming with olives, sheep, and honey-bees. And then I—a real country bumpkin—had to go and marry her, a fine city lady, a proud, luxurious lady of good family. That's the way we married, I stinking of wine dregs, and fig skins, and greasy bundles of wool, she all sweet smelling of saffron and feasting and expenses. But she was not idle, oh no, she spent money far too fast.

SERVANT: The lamp has burned up all its oil.

STREPSIADES: What? Why did you light that big lamp? Come over here and get a thrashing.

SERVANT: What for?

STREPSIADES: Because you put in a big, fat, oil-guzzling wick. Anyway, when this son was finally born to us, our heir, we began to argue about his name. She wanted to give him some knightly name: Kallippides (*Good Rider*), or Xanthippos (*Roan*), or Charippos (*Horsy Pleasure*). I wanted to call him Pheiodonides (*Thrifty*) after his grandpa. In the end we compromised on Pheidippides. She took the boy and spoiled him. She used to say: "Wait 'til you grow up and drive to the Acropolis in your purple robe like my father Megakles used to do." But I used to say: "Wait 'til you grow up and drive the goats in from the fields dressed like your father in a sheepskin coat." He never listened to me, and soon my funds were caught by a galloping consumption. Now that I have been thinking all night long, I believe I know a way out of our problems if he will follow my instructions. First, I must wake him, but sweetly and gently so that he will go along with my scheme. Pheidippides, my sweet lovely boy, wake up and kiss me and shake my hand.

PHEIDIPPIDES: Okay, Dad. What's up?

STREPSIADES: Do you love me, my son?

PHEIDIPPIDES: Of course. I swear so by Poseidon, god of horses.

STREPSIADES: No, no! Not that! Leave him out of it. That god of horses is the cause of all my troubles. But if you love me with all your heart, my son, obey me.

PHEIDIPPIDES: I shall obey.

STREPSIADES: Then change your ways immediately and go and learn what I tell you to. You see that house next door beyond the hedge? That is the thinking school of sophistic souls. There dwell men who will teach, for a price, how to speak in court and win the case whether right or wrong. I can't quite remember their names, but they are deep thinkers and fine gentlemen.

PHEIDIPPIDES: Not those cheats! I know whom you mean. Those pedants, those palefaced, barefoot tramps, Socrates and his ilk.

STREPSIADES: Sssh! Hush! Don't say those foolish things. If you care about your future estate, leave the race track, go there and learn.

PHEIDIPPIDES: What do you want me to learn?

STREPSIADES: It's well known that they keep two Logics in their school, the Better and the Worse. This second logic, the Worse, is what I want you to learn. They will teach you to speak unjustly and win. Just think, if you learn that Unjust Logic, I will never pay all the bills and debts which have been due to you and your horses, not a penny of them.

22   Sophocles, *Electra* 681-756   *ca.* 415 B.C.
The setting of this play is Mycenae where Electra plots revenge upon Klytaimnestra (her mother) and Aigisthos who had murdered her father, Agamemnon. Electra's great hope lies with her brother,

Orestes who has, unknown to her, devised the stratagem of spreading the rumor of his own death and thus lower the defenses of the murderers. Orestes' faithful paidagogos, disguised as a messenger, enters and relates the circumstances of the supposed tragedy:

Orestes went to the great festival of Greece, the Pythian Games, and when the herald announced the first contest, the foot race, he stepped forward, a radiant figure admired by all who beheld him. Like an arrow he sped from the *aphesis* to the *termata,* and took away the crown of glorious victory. To make a long story short, I never heard of such prowess. I will add this much: the judges of the games announced no contest—*diaulos, pentathlon,* and the other usual competitions—that he did not win, and each time happy cheers hailed the proclamation of the herald: "An Argive wins, Orestes son of Agamemnon, king of men and leader of the hosts of Hellas." And so things went, but when some angry god intervenes, even the strongest man is foiled.

Toward sunset the next day, he entered the chariot race. There were many charioteers: one was from Sparta, one from Achaia, two from Libya both skilled in guiding the yoked team. Orestes was the fifth in line with Thessalian mares, and an Aeolian was sixth with chestnut fillies. A Megarian was seventh; the eighth, with milkwhite steeds, was an Ainian and the ninth was from Athens, city built by the gods. Last came a Boeotian making the field of ten. They stood by while the judges cast the lots and arranged the order of the chariots. Then, at the brazen trumpet blast, they were off. All shook their reins and urged their horses on with shouts. The whole track was filled with the noise of rattling cars and the dust rose to heaven. All were bunched together and none spared the whip as each tried to break out of the pack and leave behind the whirling wheels and snorting steeds, for each saw his wheels splattered with foam and felt the breath of horses on his back. Orestes as he turned the farther *stele* held close and grazed it with the hub of his wheel, giving rein to his right horse but pulling in the nearer one. For a time all were safe and sound, but at the turn between the sixth and the seventh lap, the Ainian's horses took the bit and crashed head-on with the Libyan chariot from Barkaia. Then one after another fell into this single crash and smashed up and the whole Krisaian plain was filled with wreckage. The shrewd Athenian charioteer noted this and pulled off and slackened his pace to let the surge of panic-stricken horses pass him on the inside. Then came Orestes who had stayed behind the

pack, for he trusted in a final burst at the finish. But when he saw
that the Athenian was the one remaining rival, he shouted shrilly in
the ears of his horese and drove them on until his yoke was even with
that of the Athenian. Then the two raced on, first one, then the
other, ahead by a nose. Until now Orestes, ill-starred youth, had
taken his laps in safety, but at the last turn he loosed the left-hand
rein too soon and, without noticing it, his axle struck the *stele*. The
axle box was shattered and he was thrown over the chariot rail and,
caught in his fall by the tangle of the reins, he was dragged along
while his frightened team dashed wildly over the track. As the crowd
saw him somersault, there rose a wail of pity for the youth— for his
daring deeds and his disastrous end—while he was now bounced
into the ground, now flung head-over-heels into the sky. At last the
charioteers caught his steeds and freed the blood-stained corpse,
disfigured and marred past the recognition of his best friend.

23   Pausanias VI.20.10-19   *ca.* A.D. 170

If you leave the stadium by the place where the *Hellanodikai* sit,
you will find the region set aside for the horse races and the *aphesis*
for the horses. This *aphesis* has a shape like the prow of a ship with
its point toward the track. The prow continues up to the stoa of
Agnaptos where it has broadened. A bronze dolphin on a rod has
been made at the very tip of the point of the prow. Each side of the
aphesis is more than 400 feet in length and has stalls built into it.
Those entering the horse races are assigned stalls by lot. In front of
the chariots, or of the horses in the *keles,* is stretched a cord instead
of the *hysplex.* For each Olympiad an altar of unbaked brick,
plastered on the exterior, is made right in the middle of the prow,
and a bronze eagle with its wings stretched to the fullest extent rests
upon the altar. The official appointed for the track sets in motion
the mechanism which is inside the altar, and the eagle jumps so that
it become visible to the spectators, and the dolphin falls to the
ground. The first *hyspleges* on either side, those nearest to the stoa
of Agnaptos, let loose and the first horses stationed by them take off.
As they run they come to those who have been allotted to stand at the
second position, and at that time the second *hyspleges* let loose. The
same thing happens for all the horses so that at the tip of the prow

they should be even with one another. From this point it is up to the drivers to show their skill and to the horses to show their speed. Kleoitas was the first to devise this *aphesis,* and he seems to have been proud of it, for he inscribed the following on a statue at Athens:

He who first invented the horse *aphesis* at Olympia,
Kleoitas son of Aristokles, made me."

They say that after Kleoitas, Aristeides added some refinement to the mechanism.

One side of the hippodrome is longer than the other. The longer side is a bank of earth and, by the passageway exit through the bank, there is Taraxippos, the terror of horses. It has the shape of a circular altar, and as the horses run by it a great fear with no apparent cause seizes them. From the fear comes confusion, and in general the chariots crash and the charioteers are injured. For this reason the charioteers make sacrifices and pray that Taraxippos be kind to them. The Greeks have different views about Taraxippos. . . . It seems to me that the most probable of the stories is that Taraxippos is a surname of Poseidon of the Horses. At Isthmia Glaukos son of Sisyphos is a kind of Taraxippos. They say that he was killed by his horses when Akastos held funeral games for his father. At Nemea of the Argives there was no hero who hurt the horses, but a red rock rose up above the *kampe* of the horses, and the glare from this, as if from fire, wrought fear in the horses. But the Taraxippos at Olympia is the worst for frightening horses. On one *nyssa* is a bronze statue of Hippodameia holding a ribbon and about to crown Pelops with it for his victory.

The other side of the hippodrome is not a bank of earth, but a low hill.

24   Pausanias VI.13.9   *ca.* A.D. 170

As the Corinthians relate, the mare of the Corinthian Pheidolas was called "Breeze." At the beginning of her race, she threw her rider, but nonetheless ran on in good order and turned the *nyssa* and, when she heard the trumpet, she ran faster, finished first at the *Hellanodikai,* and, recognizing her victory, stopped running. The Eleans awarded the victory to Pheidolas and allowed him to dedicate a statue of his mare [512 B.C.].

25 *BCH, Suppl. IV* (1977) 103ff.   246 B.C.

This inscription records contracts which were let for the preparation of Delphi for the Pythian Games. Each entry has the name of a contractor, a definition of the work which he was paid to do, and the sum paid him. Broken areas on the stone where the text is not preserved are indicated within brackets.

Agazalos: digging and leveling the *xystos* and the peristyle: $296.

Agazalos: digging and leveling the *paradromis*: $200.

Agazalos: 270 bushels of white earth for the *xystos* at $2.55 per bushel: $689.

Kritolaos: fencing the *xystos*: $592.

Olympichos: maintenance work on the *xystos* and the *paradromis* and the *sphairisteria* and the gymnasion: $576.

Kritolaos: repairs to the drain alongside the shrine of Demeter: $187.

Sochares: for six picks: [?].

Euarchos: roping off the peristyle: $24.

Kleon: repairs to the wall of the *sphairisterion:* $480.

Asandros: sifting the mortar: $80.

Euthydamos: digging, leveling, and raking over the *sphairisteria:* $80.

Euthydamos: 201 bushels of black earth on the *sphairisterion* at $1.33 per bushel: $286.

Kleon: repairs to the wall by the shrine of Demeter: $472.

Pasion: plastering the *apodyterion* and the wall by the shrine of Demeter: $128.

Lyson: 15 bushels of white earth for plastering the *apodyterion* and the wall at $2.55 per bushel: $38.

Smyrnaios: cleaning out the Pythian stadium and repairing the "ridges": $176.

Smyrnaios: digging the Pythian stadium and digging and leveling the jumping pits: $1,760.

Nikon: construction of the *odeion:* $716.

Xenon: 600 bushels of white earth in the Pythian stadium at $2.22 per bushel: $1,333.

Melission: a pedestal in the Pythian theater: $448.

Euthydamos: fencing the Pythian stadium: $160.

Nikon: setting up the *proskenion* in the Pythian stadium: $96.

Nikon: the pedestal in the Pythian stadium at [?] per foot for [?]feet: $80.

Euthydamos: construction of the vaulted entrance in the Pythian
              stadium: $320.
Smyrnaios: cleaning out the [?]: $128.
Anaxagoras: construction of 36 *kampteres:* $192.
Agazalos: the [?] for the pentathletes: $144.
[?]: for 280 [?] at $3.33 each: $933.
Damastratos: [?] for the boxers: $1,240.
Melission: repair to the [?] in the vaulted entrance: $24.
[Smyrnaios]: cleaning out the hippodrome: [?].
Dionysios: digging around the *kampteres* in the hippodrome: [?].
Euthydamos: [leveling] around the *kampteres* in the hippodrome:
              $160.
Kallon: provision of tne [?] in the hippodrome: $1,264.
Dion: the [?] in the hippodrome: $608.
Dion: the [?] of the houses: $384.
Pleistos: for arbitration: [?].

26   *Eph. Arch.* (1906) 157-185   *ca.* 400 B.C. ?
*The following regulation is inscribed on the side of the retaining wall
of the stadium at Delphi about 50 feet from the southeast entrance.
The forms of the carved letters suggest a date in the late fifth century
B.C. There are difficulties with a few details, but the general
significance of the regulation is clear.*

   Wine is prohibited in the vicinity of the track. If anyone breaks
this rule, he shall make amends to Apollo by pouring a libation,
making a sacrifice, and paying a fine of $40, half to Apollo and half
to the informer.

27   Lucian, *Anacharsis* 9-14   [*ca.* 590 B.C.]
See above, no. 9
ANACHARSIS: What are these prizes for which you compete?
SOLON: A crown of olive at Olympia, a crown of pine at
Isthmia, a crown of wild celery at Nemea, the laurel-berries sacred to
Apollo at Delphi, and the oil of the olive at the Panathenaia. Why
are you laughing, Anacharsis? Do you think that these prizes are in-
significant?

ANACHARSIS: Oh no, Solon, the prizes which you listing are most imposing. I am sure that those who offer them take pride in their generosity, and that the contestants are most eager to carry them off. So much so that they are willing to undergo these preliminary pains and to risk getting choked and broken in two by one another in order to get some laurel-berries and celery, as if it were not possible for anyone who wants them to get laurel-berries in large quantities, or to wear a crown of celery or of pine without getting his face smeared with mud or his belly kicked by the opposition.

SOLON: But my good man, we do not look at the mere prizes which are handed out. They are tokens of victory and a way to recognize the victors. Together with them goes a reputation which is worth everything to the victors, and getting kicked is a small price to pay for those who seek fame through pain. It cannot be acquired without pain, and the man who wants it must endure many hardships in the beginning before he can even start to see the profitable and sweet end of his efforts.

ANACHARSIS: When you speak of a 'profitable and sweet end,' Solon, you mean that everyone will see them wearing crowns and congratulate them on their victory after having pitied them for a long time during their pains, and that they will be fortunate to have traded in their pains for laurel-berries and celery?

SOLON: You are still ignorant of our customs, I tell you. In a little while you will change your mind when you go to the games and see that huge crowd of people gathering to see such things, and the theaters filled with thousands, and the contestants cheered, and he who wins thought equal to the gods.

ANACHARSIS: That is just the worst of it, Solon, if they have to endure these things not in front of a few, but before so many spectators and witnesses of the brutality. The latter probably congratulate the contestants upon seeing them streaming with blood or being strangled by their opponents, for these are the companions of their victories. With us Skythians, Solon, anyone who strikes a citizen or throws him down, or tears his clothing gets a severe penalty from the elders even if the offense was witnessed by just a few, not to speak of the huge crowds which you describe at Isthmia and Olympia. I cannot but pity the competitors for what they endure, and I am amazed at the spectators who you say come from everywhere to the festivals, and are noble and prominent men but neglect their own urgent business for such things. I am unable to understand what pleasure it is to them to see men beaten, and slapped around, and smashed to the ground, and crushed by one another.

SOLON: If it were the time, Anacharsis, for the Olympic or Isthmian or Panathenaic Games, the events there would have taught you that we have not wasted our time on this subject. I cannot, just by telling you about it, convince you of the pleasure of what happens at such a festival as well as you would learn for yourself, sitting in the middle of the crowd, watching the *arete* of men and physical beauty, amazing conditioning and great skill and irresistible force and daring and pride and unbeatable determination and indescribable passion for victory. I know that you would not stop praising and cheering and applauding.

ANACHARSIS: No doubt, Solon, and laughing and jeering as well. I see that all these things—*arete* and conditioning and beauty and daring—are a waste since there is no purpose to them. It would be different if your country were in danger or your farmlands being raided or your friends and family being brutally kidnapped. Thus the competitors are all the more ridiculous if, as you say, they are the flower of the country and yet endure so much for nothing, making themselves wretched and marring their great big beautiful bodies with sand and black eyes in order that they might get a laurel-berry and an olive branch. I like to keep mentioning the prizes because they are so wonderful. But tell me, do all the contestants receive them?

SOLON: Not at all. Only one among them—the victor.

28   *IG* II² 2311   400-350 B.C.

This inscription contains a list of the prizes awarded in the Panathenaic Games at some point during the first half of the fourth century B.C. Although much of the original text is broken away, enough remains to reveal many of the prizes. Because of the differing nature of these, the estimated dollar value is given in parentheses next to the actual prize. Before the heading "For the Warriors," all competitions were open to any Greeks, after that heading the competitions were open only to Athenian citizens competing as individuals or as members of their tribe's teams. It may be noted that the total of the estimated value of the prizes, in excess of $120,000, does not include many parts which are broken *away, especially the prizes for all of the athletic competitions in the men's category and nearly all of the equestrian events. Broken areas on the stone where the text is not preserved are indicated with brackets.*

For the Kithara-singers:

First Place: a crown of olive in gold weighing
1,000 drachmai ($8,000) and 500 silver drachmai
($4,000).

Second place: 1,200 drachmai ($9,600).

Third place: 600 drachmai ($4,800).

Fourth place: 400 drachmai ($3,200).

Fifth place: 300 drachmai ($2,400).

For the Flute-singers in the Men's Category:

First place: a crown weighing 300 drachmai ($2,400).

Second place: 100 drachmai ($800).

For the Kitharists in the Men's Category:

First place: a crown weighing 300 drachmai ($2,400) and
500 drachmai ($4,000).

Second place: [3]00 drachmai ($2,400).

Third place: 100 drachmai ($800).

For the Flute players:

First place: a crown weighing [?].

several lines missing on the stone

For the Victor in the Stadion in the Boy's Category:

50 amphoras of olive oil ($4,800).

Second place: 10 amphoras of olive oil ($960).

For the Victor in the Pentathlon in the Boy's Category:

30 amphoras of olive oil ($2,880).

Second place: 6 amphoras of olive oil ($576).

For the Victor in the Wrestling in the Boy's Category:

30 amphoras of olive oil ($2,880).

Second place: 6 amphoras of olive oil ($576).

For the Victor in the Boxing in the Boy's Category:

30 amphoras of olive oil ($2,880).

Second place: 6 amphoras of olive oil ($576).

For the Victor in the Pankration in the Boy's Category:

40 amphoras of olive oil ($3,840).

Second place: 8 amphoras of olive oil ($768).

For the Victor in the Stadion in the *Ageneios* Category:

60 amphoras of olive oil ($5,760).

Second place: 12 amphoras of olive oil ($1,152).
For the Victor in the Pentathlon in the *Ageneios* Category:
   40 amphoras of olive oil ($3,840).
   Second place: 8 amphoras of olive oil ($768).
For the Victor in the Wrestling in the *Ageneios* Category:
   40 amphoras of olive oil ($3,840).
   Second place: 8 amphoras of olive oil ($768).
For the Victor in the Boxing in the *Ageneios* Category:
   40 amphoras of olive oil ($3,840).
   Second place: 8 amphoras of olive oil ($768).
For the Victor [in the Pankration in the *Ageneios* Category]:
   [50 amphoras of olive oil ($4,800)].
   [Second Place: 10 amphoras of olive oil ($960)].
                  Several lines missing on the stone
For the Two-Horse Chariot Race in the Foal's Category:
   40 amphoras of olive oil ($3,840).
   Second place: 8 amphoras of olive oil ($768).
For the Two-Horse Chariot Race in the Full Grown Category:
   140 amphoras of olive oil ($13,440).
   Second place: 40 amphoras of olive oil ($3,840).

FOR THE WARRIORS:

For the Victor in the *Keles*:
   16 amphoras of olive oil ($1,536).
   Second place: 4 amphoras of olive oil ($384).
For the Victor in the Two-Horse Chariot Race:
   30 amphoras of olive oil ($2,880).
   Second place: 6 amphoras of olive oil ($576).
For the Victor in the Processional Two-Horse Chariot:
   4 amphoras of olive oil ($384).
   Second place ($96).
For the Hurler of the Javelin from Horseback:
   5 amphoras of olive oil ($480).
   1 amphora of olive oil ($96).
For the War Dancers in the Boy's Category:
   A bull and 100 drachmai ($800).
For the War Dancers in the *Ageneios* Category:
   A bull and 100 drachmai ($800).
For the War Dancers in the Men's Category:
   A bull and 100 drachmai ($800).

For the Winning Tribe in Physical Fitness:
  A bull and 100 drachmai ($800).
For the Winning Tribe in the Torch Race:
  A bull and 100 drachmai ($800).
For the Individual Victor in the Torch Race:
  30 water jars.
PRIZES FOR THE BOAT RACE:
For the winning tribe: 3 bulls and 300 drachmai ($2,400) and
  200 free meals.
Second place: 2 bulls and 200 drachmai ($1,600).
The rest of the stone is broken away

29   Pausanias V.24.9-10   *ca.* A.D. 170

Of all the images of Zeus, the Zeus in the *Bouleuterion* is the one most likely to strike terror into the hearts of sinners. This Zeus is surnamed Horkios [of the Oath], and he holds a thunderbolt in each hand. Beside this statue it is established for the athletes, their fathers and brothers, and their trainers to swear an oath on slices of the flesh of wild boars that they will do nothing evil against the Olympic Games. The athletes in the men's category also swear in addition that they have adhered strictly to their training for ten successive months. Those who judge the ages of the boys and of the foals entered in the competitions also swear that they will judge fairly and without taking bribes, and they will guard in secrecy everything about the examinee. I did not remember to ask what has to be done with the wild boar's meat after the oath of the athletes, although in more ancient times it was established with regard to sacrificial victims that a human being might not eat of that upon which an oath had been sworn.

30   Philostratos, *Life of Apollonius* V.43   *ca.* A.D. 70
This Philostratos, probably the same as the author of the treatise on gymnastics (see above, nos. 5, 7, and 15), wrote in the early third century after Christ a biography of Apollonius of Tyana who was a

religious and philosophical leader who was teaching slightly later than Christ. Indeed, both holy men were worshipped, together with Orpheus, Abraham, and Alexander the Great by the Emperor Alexander Severus (A.D. 205-235). The setting for this passage is Alexandria which Apollonius is about to leave for a visit to a sect of "naked prophets" on the upper Nile. As a part of his preparations for the journey, Apollonius calls together his followers and addresses them:

This undertaking requires an Olympic exordium, my men, which might be as follows. When the Olympic festival is approaching, the Eleans train the athletes for thirty days in Elis itself. Likewise, the people of Delphi collect the athletes when the Pythian festival approaches, and the Corinthians for the Isthmian festival, and they say to the athletes: "Go now into the stadium, and be men worthy of winning." When they are going to Olympia, however, the Eleans say to the athletes: "If you have worked so as to be worthy of going to Olympia, if you have done nothing indolent nor ignoble, then take heart and march on; but those who have not so trained may leave and go wherever they like."

31   *POxy* II.222   *ca.* A.D. 250

This document is a fragment of papyrus which was found in Egypt late in the last century. Although written in the third century after Christ, it contains a list of the victors in the Olympic Games from the fifth century before Christ. Where it can be checked against other evidence, it reveals itself to be very accurate. It shows not only the nature of the Olympic victors' list, but also how widespread and easily attainable such information was in antiquity. We can only regret that we do not have more of it. Areas where the papyrus is torn away and the text not preserved are indicated in brackets.

Xenopithes of Chios, the *stadion* in the boys' category.

[. . .]kon of Argos, the *pale* in the boys' category.

[. . .]phanes of Heraia, the *pyx* in the boys' category.

[Ast]ylos of Syracuse, the *hoplites*.

[. . .]tondas and Arsilochos of Thebes, the *tethrippon*.

[Arg]os public, the *keles*.

[The 76th Olympiad 476 B.C.]

[Ska]mandros of Mitylene, the *stadion*.

[Da]ndis of Argos, the *diaulos*.

[?] of Sparta, the *dolichos*.

[?] of Taras, the *pentathlon*.

[?] of Maroneia, the *pale*.

[Euthymos of Lok]roi in Italy, the *pyx*.

[Theagenes of Th]asos, the *pankration*.

[? of S]parta, the *stadion* in the boys' category.

[Theognetos of Aigi]na, the *pale* in the boys' category.

[Ag]lesi[da]mos of Lokroi in Italy, the *pyx* in the boys' category.

[Ast]ylos of Syracuse, the *hoplites*.

[Ther]on of Akragas, the *tethrippon*.

[Hier]on of Syracuse, the *keles*.

[The 77th Olympiad 472 B.C.]

[Dan]dis of Argos, the *stadion*.

[. . .]ges of Epidauros, the *diaulos*.

[Erg]oteles of Himera, the *dolichos*.

[. . .]amos of Miletos, the *pentathlon*.

[. . .]menes of Samos, the *pale*.

[Euth]ymos of Lokroi in Italy, the *pyx*.

[Ka]llias of Athens, the *pankration*.

[. . .]tandridas of Corinth, the *stadion* in the boys' category.

[. . .]kratidas of Taras, the *pale* in the boys' category.

[Tel]lon of Mainalos, the *pyx* in the boys' category.

[. . .]gias of Epidamnos, the *hoplites*.

[Arg]os public, the *tethrippon*.

[Hier[on of Syracuse, the *keles*.

[The 78th Olympiad 468 B.C.]

[P]armeneides of Poseidonia, the *stadion*.

[Par]meneides, the same, the *diaulos*.

[. . .]medes, of Sparta, the *dolichos*.

[. . .]tion of Taras, the *pentathlon*.

[Epha]rmostos of Opous, the *pale*.

[Me]nalkes of Opous, the *pyx*.

[. .]titimadas of Argos, the *pankration*.

[Lyk]ophron of Athens, the *stadion* in the boys' category.

[. . .]emos of Parrhasia, the *pale* in the boys' category.

[. . .]los of Athens, the *hoplites*.

[. . .]nymos of Syracuse, the *tethrippon*.

the papyrus breaks off

32   Lucian, *Herodotus* 1-4 and 7-8   [*ca.* 430 B.C.]

Lucian (see above, no. 9) presented this essay before an audience in
Macedonia, which he compares and contrasts to Olympia. In so
doing he provides us with a glimpse of the non-athletic activities
which went on at a Panhellenic festival.

Would that some of the other qualities of Herodotus could be
imitated. I do not mean all of them, for this would be too much to
hope for, but just one of them, perhaps the beauty of his diction, or
the harmony of his words, the aptness of expression native to Ionia,
or his extraordinary judgement, or of the countless diverse elements
which he has brought together into a unity beyond hope of imitation.
One quality, however, which you and I and everyone else can imitate
is in the handling of his composition and in the speed with which he
developed his reputation throughout the whole Greek world.

When he had sailed from his home in Caria straight to Greece, he
considered what would be the quickest and easiest route to fame and
reputation for himself and his writings. He thought that it would be
a long and tedious waste of time to travel around reading his works,
now in Athens, now in Corinth or Argos, now in Sparta. He had no
appetite for such a hit-and-miss proposition which would, moreover,
delay his acquisition of a reputation, and he planned to win the
hearts of all the Greeks at a single point in time if he could.

The time for the Olympic festival was approaching, and
Herodotus thought that this was the opportunity for which he had
been waiting. He kept an eye out at the festival until it was crowded
and the most prominent men had assembled from everywhere. Then
he went into the rear chamber of the Temple of Zeus not like a
spectator, but like a contestant in the Olympic Games. He then
recited his histories and so mesmerized those present that his books
were called after the Muses, since they were also nine in number.

It was not long until he was better known than the Olympic
victors. There was not a man who had not heard the name of
Herodotus; some heard it at Olympia, others heard it from those
returning from the festival. All he had to do was appear and
someone would point him out: "That there is Herodotus who wrote in
Ionic of the Persian Wars and celebrated our victories." Such were
the rewards of his histories that in a single assembly he won the
universal acclaim of the whole Greece and he was proclaimed not
just by a single herald, but in every city-state which had some
participant at the festival.

Those who followed learned the lesson of this short-cut to fame. Hippias the sophist, who was a native of Elis, and Prodikos of Keos and Anaximenes of Chios and Polos of Akragas and dozens of others always recited their works in person at the festivals and thus won quick recognition.

But there is no need for me to talk about those ancient sophists and authors since more recently Aetion the painter displayed his own painting of the "Marriage of Roxane and Alexander" at Olympia. Proxenides, a *Hellanodikes* at the time, was so enthusiastic about his talent that he married his daughter to Aetion.

Herodotus, to return to him, thought that the Olympic festival was a suitable place for him, the displayer of Greek victories, to be displayed to the Greeks. Please do not think that I am mad or that I compare my works to his, but he and I are similar. When I first came to stay in Macedonia, I wondered what to do. My first desire was to become known to all of you and to show off my works to the most Macedonians possible, but to go around at that time of the year in person to each city seemed less than convenient. Rather, I thought to await your present festival and make my appearance to deliver my lecture. Thus, I thought, would my prayers be answered.

Now you are all assembled together, the heads of each city, the leaders of Macedonia, in the fairest of all cities which is not, thank goodness, like Olympia with its cramped quarters, its tents and shanties, and its stifling heat. Nor is my audience a crude crowd which would rather be watching athletes than hearing Herodotus. It is the best of orators and historians and sophists. If you compare me to Polydamas, or Glaukos, or Milo, you will think that I am a fool-hardy man. But if you forget them and strip me and look at me alone, I shall not seem so deserving of the whip. But even such a judgement would be satisfactory in such a stadium.

33   Dio Chrysostom VIII. 4-6, 9-12, 26, 36   [ca. 359 B.C.]
Dio the "Golden Mouthed" was an orator and philosopher who was no stranger to the panhellenic games. In A.D. 97 he delivered a speech at the Olympic Games, and in this discourse he portrayed the Cynic philosopher Diogenes at the Isthmian Games. We cannot be certain whether the picture of the festival is to be taken as true to the time of Diogenes or to that of Dio four centuries later; perhaps there was little difference.

After the death of his friend Antisthenes, Diogenes moved from Athens to Corinth, and he lived there without either renting a house or staying with a friend. He camped out in a public park. The reason for his move was that he observed that most men visited Corinth at one time or another because of its harbors and prostitutes, and because the city was located at the cross-roads of Greece. Thus, just as the good doctor will go to help where the largest number of sick people are, so Diogenes thought it was necessary for the wise man to go where fools proliferate.

When the time came for the Isthmian Games, and everyone was at Isthmia, he went too. It was his custom at the festivals to study the ambitions of men and why they went out in public and what it was that was a source of pride to them.

That was also the time to hear crowds of wretched sophists around the Temple of Poseidon as they shouted and heaped abuse on each other, and their so-called students as they fought with one another, and many historians reading out their dumb writings, and many poets reciting their poetry to the applause of others, and many magicians showing their tricks, many fortune-tellers telling fortunes, countless lawyers perverting justice, and not a few peddlers peddling whatever came to hand. Immediately a crowd gathered around him too, but with no Corinthians since they saw him every day in Corinth and had grown accustomed to the novelty. Thus, the crowd consisted of strangers, and each of them would speak or listen for a short time and then leave, fearing his examination of their opinions. For this reason Diogenes said that he was like a Laconian dog; many men would pet these dogs and play with them when they were displayed at the festivals, but no one would buy one because no one knew how to handle them.

When one man asked Diogenes if he too had come to watch the competition, Diogenes said, "No, but to participate." When the man laughed and asked him who his competitors were, Diogenes gave him his familiar glowering glance and said: "The toughest and most difficult to defeat, ones which no Greek can stare down. Not those competitors who run or wrestle or jump, nor those who box and throw the javelin and the diskos, but those who chastise a man." "Who are they?" asked the other. "Hardships," said Diogenes, "which are severe and unbeatable for men who are gluttons and puffed with their own worth and snore at night, but which can be conquered by men who are thin and lean and have waists thinner than wasps. Or do you think that those pot-bellied bullies are good for something? I think that they are ripe candidates to serve as sacrificial victims and that they have less soul than swine. The man who is noble is the one who considers hardship as his greatest competitor and struggles with it day and night, and not, like some goat, for a bit of celery or olive or pine, but for the sake of happiness and *arete* throughout his whole life.

Diogenes continues with this theme for some time, explaining more fully his meaning and drawing upon mythology, especially upon the labors of Herakles, to illustrate his point.

While Diogenes was saying these things, many people collected around him and listened with great pleasure. Then, perhaps with the thought of Herakles and the Augean stables still in his mind, he stopped speaking, squatted on the ground, and performed an indecent act. At this the crowd scattered, saying that he was crazy, and the sophists raised their din again.

34   Lucian, *Peregrinus* 19-21, 31-32, 35-37   A.D. 165

The following is excerpted from a letter in which Lucian describes to a friend an extraordinary happening at the Olympic Games of A.D. 165. This involved one Peregrinus, or Proteus as he was also known, a Cynic philosopher who had converted to Christianity in his early life, reverted to Cynicism, and then became enamoured of Indian mysticism. Lucian clearly had no great love for him. These passages show, of course, the lengths to which some were willing to go to attract attention to themselves, but they also reveal something of the activities which went on, at least in the Roman period, before and after the Olympic festival proper. The opening scene is set in a gymnasium at Elis and the speaker (perhaps Lucian himself) is rebutting a disciple of Peregrinus who had just previously spoken. He recounts the career of Peregrinus.

Coming at last to Greece when he had been sent packing from Rome, he arrived at Olympia (*A.D. 153*) where at one moment he abused the Eleans, the next he tried to incite the Greeks to rebel against Rome, and the next he libelled a man who was not only outstanding in literary achievements but also prominent because of his many benefactions to Greece (*Herodes Atticus*). Peregrinus attacked him particularly because he had brought water to Olympia and prevented the visitors to the festival from dying of thirst. Peregrinus accused him of making the Greeks soft, for the spectators of the Olympic Games ought to endure their thirst and—yes by Zeus—even die on account of the dryness of the place. And he said these things while he drank the very same water.

When the crowd stoned him with one accord and nearly killed him, Peregrinus—stout chap—managed to escape death by hiding in the Temple of Zeus. Afterwards, at the next Olympiad (*A.D. 157*), he delivered to the Greeks a speech which he had composed during the intervening four years. In this he praised the man who had brought in the water and defended himself for running away at that time.

Finally, he came to be scorned by all and no longer admired, for his stuff was all old-hat and he could find no further novelty with which to surprise those who came his way, and make them marvel and stare at him. So he concocted this ultimate bit of recklessness about the pyre and spread a story among the Greeks immediately after the last Olympic festival (*A.D. 161*) that he would burn himself up at the next festival. And now, they say, the faker is actually doing this, digging a pit, collecting firewood, and promising some fantastic endurance.

The speaker goes on for some time, disparaging Peregrinus and his followers, and inciting the crowd against them. He then leaves the platform at the approach of one of those disciples.

When Theagenes heard the shouting, he came at once, got up, and began to rant and shout countless terrible things about the man who had just got down—I do not know the name of that excellent man. I left him busting his gut and went off to the athletes, for the *Hellanodikai* were said to be already in the room where they matched the athletes by lot.

That is what happened at Elis. When we reached Olympia, the rear chamber of the Temple of Zeus was full of people either criticizing Proteus or praising his goal, and most of them came to blows. Finally, Proteus himself, together with a huge crowd, appeared after the contest for the heralds. He had, of course, something to say about himself, telling of his life and the risks which he had run and of all the difficulties which he had endured for the sake of philosophy. He had a great deal to say, but I heard little of it due to the number of bystanders. In the end I was afraid of being crushed

in the confusion, and I left bidding a long farewell to the sophist who
was so enamoured of death as to be delivering his own funeral
oration.

*Lucian goes on to recount a little of Peregrinus' speech and some-
thing of his satisfaction at the admiring crowd which he had excited.*

The end of the Olympic Games soon came—the best Olympics
which I have seen incidentally, of the four which I have attended as a
spectator. It was not easy to get a carriage since so many were
leaving at that time, and so I stayed on against my will. Meanwhile,
Peregrinus kept delaying, but finally announced a night upon which
he would cremate himself. One of my companions invited me to go
along, and so I rose at midnight and took the road to Harpina where
the pyre was. This is nearly three and a half miles from Olympia as
you leave by the hippodrome toward the east. As soon as we arrived
we found a pyre laid in a pit about six feet deep. It was made mostly
of the pitchy wood of torches, with brush in the gaps so that it would
ignite quickly. When the moon was rising (she also had to see this
greatest of deeds) he approached, dressed as usual, and with him
were the leaders of the Cynics. Proteus, and some of the others, held
a torch. Coming forward from all sides, they lit a huge fire.
Peregrinus, laying aside his wallet, his cloak, and that Herakles'
club, stood there in an absolutely filthy shirt. Then he asked for
incense to throw on the fire. When someone produced it, he threw it
into the burning pyre, and then faced south and said: "Shades of my
mother and my father, receive me kindly." Having said this, he
jumped into the fire. He was not, however, visible for he was
surrounded by the flames which had risen to a considerable height.

I did not criticize him for calling upon the spirit of his mother, but
I could not restrain my laughter when he called upon the spirit of his
father, for I remembered the stories that he had killed his father.
The Cynics stood around the pyre, not weeping, but their silence
showing some grief as they watched the fire. Finally choked with
rage at them, I said: "Let's leave, you fools. Its no fun to look at a
roasted old man nor to pick up that vile odor on ourselves. Or are
you waiting for some painter to come along and portray you as the
companions of Socrates in prison are portrayed?" They were
beside themselves and reviled me and some even went for their
walking sticks. But then, after I threatened to gather up some of
them and throw them into the fire so that they could follow their
teacher, they shut up and kept quiet.

35   Pausanias V.6.7-8   *ca.* A.D. 170

As one goes from Skillos down the road to Olympia, but before one crosses the Alpheios river, there is a mountain with high and very steep cliffs. The name of the mountain is Typaion. The Eleans have a law to throw off these cliffs any women who are discovered at the Olympic festival, or even on the Olympia side of the Alpheios on the days which are forbidden to women. They say that no woman has ever been caught except Kallipateira. (Some say that the name of the woman was Pherenike, not Kallipateira.) She had been widowed and, disguised like a male trainer, she took her son to Olympia to compete. When her son Peisirodos won, Kallipateira jumped over the fence with which the trainers were restrained, and exposed herself. She was thus discovered to be a woman, but they released her unpunished out of respect for her father (*Diagoras of Rhodes, see below, no. 81*), her brothers, and her son all of whom had been victors at Olympia. They passed a law, however, that in the future trainers would have to attend the competition in the nude.

36   Pausanias VI.20.8-9   *ca.* A.D. 170

The stadium is a bank of earth on which is a seat for the sponsors of the competition. Opposite the *Hellanodikai* is an altar of white marble. Seated on this a woman watched the Olympic Games, the priestess of Demeter Chamyne; this office is bestowed on a woman from time to time by the Eleans. They do not prevent virgins from watching the games.

37   Pausanias III.8.1   *ca.* A.D. 170

The Spartan King Archidamos had a daughter whose name was Kyniska. She was extremely ambitious to enter the competition at Olympia, and was the first woman to breed horses and the first woman to win an Olympic victory. Other women, especially Lacedaimonian women, won Olympic victories after Kyniska, but none is so famous as she.

38   Pausanias V.16.2-8   *ca.* A.D. 170

Every fourth year at Olympia the Sixteen Women weave a robe for
Hera, and they also sponsor the Heraia competition. This contest is a
foot race for virgins who are of different ages. They run in three
categories: the youngest first, the slightly older ones next, and then
the oldest virgins are the last to run. They run as follows: their hair
hangs down on them, a chiton reaches to a little above the knee, and
the right shoulder is bared as far as the breast. They also use the
Olympic stadium, but the track is shortened by one-sixth. The
winners receive a crown of olive and a portion of the cow sacrificed to
Hera, and they have the right to dedicate statues with their names
inscribed upon them. Those who serve the Sixteen Women are, like
the sponsors of these games, women. They trace the competition of
the virgins also back to antiquity. They say that Hippodameia, out of
gratitude to Hera for her marriage to Pelops, collected Sixteen
Women and, with them, sponsored the first Heraia. ... The
Sixteen Women also arrange two choral dances; they call one that of
Physkoa, the other that of Hippodameia. ... The Eleans are now
divided into eight tribes, and from each they choose two women.
Neither the Sixteen Women nor the *Hellanodikai* perform their
established rituals until they have purified themselves with a pig
which is suitable for purification and with water. This purification
takes place at the spring called Piera which is by the plain going
from Olympia to Elis.

39   *SIG*³ 802   A.D. 47

*The following inscription was found at Delphi on a limestone
statue base which originally supported the statue of three sisters.*

Hermesianax son of Dionysios, citizen of Kaisarea Tralles as well
as of Athens and Delphi, dedicates this to Pythian Apollo on behalf
of his daughters who hold the same citizenships:

for Tryphosa, who won the Pythian Games when Antigonos and
Kleomachidas were *agonothetai,* and the following Isthmian Games
when Iouventios Proklos was *agonothetes,* in the *stadion,* first of the
virgins.

for Hedea, who won the chariot race in armor at the Isthmian

Games when Cornelius Pulcher was *agonothetes,* and the *stadion* at
the Nemean Games when Antigonos was *agonothetes* and at Sikyon
when Menoitas was *agonothetes.* She also won the kithara-singing in
the boys' category at the Sebasteia in Athens when Nouios son of
Philinos was *agonothetes.*

for Dionysia, who won the Isthmian Games when Antigonos was
agonothetes and the games of Asklepios at sacred Epidauros when
Nikoteles was *agonothetes,* in the *stadion.*

40   Pausanias VI.14.5-8   *ca.* A.D. 170
Dameas of Kroton made the statue of Milo son of Diotimos also of
Kroton. Milo won six victories in the *pale* at Olympia, including one
in the boys' category (*536 B.C.*). At Delphi he won six times in the
men's category and once in the boys'. He came to Olympia to wrestle
for the seventh time (*in 512 B.C.*), but he could not beat his fellow
citizen Timasitheos who was younger than he and who refused to
come to close quarters with him. It is also said that Milo carried his
own statue into the *Altis,* and there are stories about him concerning
the pomegranate and the diskos. He would grip a pomegranate so
that no one could wrest it away and yet not squeeze it so hard as to
bruise it. He would stand upon a greased diskos and make fools out
of those who would rush at him and try to knock him off the diskos.
There were other things which he did to show off. He would tie a
cord around his forehead as if it were a ribbon or a crown. He would
then hold his breath until the veins in his head were filled with blood
and then break the cord by the strength of those veins. Another story
is that he would let his right arm hang down along his side to the
elbow, but turn his forearm out at right angles with the thumb up
and the fingers in a row stretched out straight so that the little finger
was the lowest, and no could force the little finger away from the
other fingers. They say that he was killed by wild beasts. In the land
of Kroton he happened upon a dried up tree trunk into which
wedges had been placed to split it. Milo, in his vanity, stuck his
hands into the trunk, the wedges slipped, and Milo was caught in the
trunk until wolves discovered him.

41   Athenaeus, *The Gastronomers* X.412F   *ca.* A.D. 228
Milo of Kroton used to eat twenty pounds of meat and twenty

pounds of bread and wash it down with eight quarts of wine. At
Olympia he hoisted a four year old bull on his shoulders and carried
it around the stadium, and then butchered it and ate it all alone in
one day.

42   Pausanias VI.9.6-7   *ca.* A.D. 170

It is said that at the Olympic festival in 492 B.C. Kleomedes of
Astypalaia killed Ikkos of Epidauros during the boxing. When he
was convicted by the *Hellanodikai* of foul play and stripped of his
victory, he went out of his mind with grief and returned to
Astypalaia. Once there he attacked a school with about sixty
children in it and pulled down the column which supported the roof
which fell on the children. When the townspeople came after him
with rocks and stones, he took refuge in the sanctuary of Athena
where he hid in a box with the lid closed over him. Try as they might,
the Astypalaians could not open the box. Finally, they smashed the
boards of the box, but found neither Kleomedes nor his corpse.
Puzzled by this, they sent representatives to Delphi to ask what had
happened to Kleomedes. The Pythia, they say, responded in the
following way:

Kleomedes of Astypalaia is the last of heroes.

Honor with sacrifices him who is no longer mortal.

From that time the Astypalaians worshipped Kleomedes as a
hero.

43   Pausanias VI.6.4-6   *ca.* A.D. 170

Euthymos was born in the land of the Lokrians in Italy; they live
near the Zephyrian cape. His father was called Astykles, but the
locals say that he was the son, not of this man, but of the river
Kaikinos which divides the territory of Lokris from that of Rhegion.
Although Euthymos won the victory in boxing in the 74th Olympiad
(*484 B.C.*), he was not successful at the next Olympiad. The reason
was that Theagenes of Thasos wanted to win at one Olympiad both
the boxing and the *pankration*. He beat Euthymos in the boxing, but

did not have enough strength left to win the olive in the *pankration* because he was already exhausted by his fight with Euthymos. For this the *Hellanodikai* penalized Theagenes with a fine of $48,000 to be paid to Zeus, and another $48,000 to be paid to Euthymos. They judged that Theagenes had entered the boxing merely to spite Euthymos. At the 76th Olympiad (*476 B.C.*) Theagenes paid in full the fine to Zeus, and did not enter the boxing competition as compensation to Euthymos. In this Olympiad, and again in the next (*472 B.C.*), Euthymos won the crown in boxing.
(*see above, no. 31*)

44   Pausanias VI.11.2-9   *ca.* A.D. 170
    The next statue at Olympia is that of Theagenes the son of Timosthenes of Thasos. The Thasians, however, say that Theagenes was not the son of Timosthenes, who was a priest of the Thasian Herakles, but of a phantom of Herakles which, disguised as Timosthenes, had intercourse with Theagenes' mother. They say that when Theagenes was nine years old, as he was going home from school, the bronze statue of some god which stood in the agora caught his fancy, so he picked up the statue, put it on his shoulders, and carried it home. The citizens were outraged by what he had done, but one of their respected elders convinced them not to kill the boy, but to order him to go home immediately and bring the statue back to the agora. He did this and quickly became famous for his strength as his feat was shouted through the length and breadth of Greece. I have already related the most famous of Theagenes' achievements at Olympia (*above, no. 43*). It was then for the first time in the records that the *pankration* was won *akoniti*; the victor was Dromeus of Mantineia. At the next festival (*476 B.C.*), Theagenes won the *pankration*. He also won three times at Delphi in the boxing. His nine victories at Nemea and ten at Isthmia were divided between the boxing and the *pankration*. At Phthia in Thessaly he ceased training for the boxing and the *pankration*, but concentrated upon winning fame among the Greeks for his running, and he defeated those who entered in the *dolichos*. He won a total of 1,400 victories. After he died, one of his enemies came every night to the statue of Theagenes in Thasos, and flogged the bronze image as though he were whipping Theagenes himself. The statue stopped

this outrage by falling upon the man, but his sons prosecuted the statue for murder. The Thasians threw the statue into the sea, following the precepts of Drako who, when he wrote the homicide laws for the Athenians, imposed banishment even upon inanimate objects which fell and killed a man. As time went by, however, famine beset the Thasians and they sent envoys to Delphi. Apollo instructed them to recall their exiles. They did so, but there was still no end to the famine. They sent to the Pythia for a second time and said that, although they had followed the instructions, the wrath of the gods still was upon them. The Pythia then responded to them:

You do not remember your great Theagenes.

The Thasians were then in a quandry, for they could not think how to retrieve the statue of Theagenes. But fishermen, who had set out for fish, happened to catch the statue in their nets and brought it back to land. The Thasians set the statue back up in its original position, and are now accustomed to sacrifice to Theagenes as to a god. I know of many places, both among the Greeks and among the barbarians where statues of Theagenes have been set up. He is worshipped by the natives as a healing power.

45 *BCH* 64-65 (1940-41) p. 175   *ca.* A.D. 100
This inscription was discovered at Thasos outside the shrine of the heroized Theagenes. It is inscribed upon a marble block which has a large cavity hollowed out of its center with a connecting slit to the top surface of the block; in other words, an offering box.

Those who sacrifice to Theogenes are to contribute not less than $3 in the offering box. Anyone who does not make a contribution as written above will be remembered. The money collected each year is to be given to the High Priest, and he is to save it until it has reached a total of $16,000. When this total has been collected, the *Boule* and the People shall decide whether it is to be spent for some ornamentation or for repairs to the shrine of Theogenes.

46   Pausanias X.9.2   *ca.* A.D. 170
Most men take no account of the competitors in the musical

contests, and I think that they are not worth much trouble. Moreover, I have already discussed those athletes who are famous in my
account of Elis. At Delphi there is, however, a statue of Phaÿlos of
Kroton. He had no victories at Olympia, but at Delphi he won twice
in the *pentathlon* (*482 and 478 B.C.*) and a third victory in the
stadion. He fought against the Persians at sea (*480 B.C.*) in his own
ship which he equipped at his own expense and manned with fellow
citizens from Kroton who were living in Greece. Such is the story of
the athlete from Kroton.

47   *Anth. Pal.* App. 297   [482 B.C.]
   Phaÿlos jumped fifty feet plus five, but he threw the diskos one
hundred feet minus five.

48   Pausanias VI.5.1-9   *ca.* A.D. 170
   The statue on a high base is the work of Lysippos, and it is of the
tallest of all men except those called heroes. . . . Other men have
won glorious victories in the *pankration,* but Polydamas the son of
Nikias of Skotoussa has other feats to his credit in addition to his
crowns for the *pankration* (*including one at Olympia in 408 B.C.*).
The mountainous region of Thrace which lies on this side of the
Nestos river as it flows through the land of Abdera breeds many wild
beasts including lions. The lions frequently roam as far south as the
region around Mt. Olympos one side of which faces north toward
Macedonia, the other south toward Thessaly and the Peneios river.
On this part of Mt. Olympos Polydamas killed a lion, a huge and
powerful wild beast, without the use of a weapon. His ambition to
rival the labors of Herakles drove him to do this, for Herakles also
killed the lion of Nemea according to the legend. Polydamas also
went into a herd of cattle and grabbed the largest and strongest bull
by one of its hind feet. Polydamas held the hoof fast despite the
bull's leaps and struggles until it finally put forth all its strength and
escaped, but left its hoof behind in the hand of Polydamas. It is also
said of him that he stopped a charioteer who was driving his chariot
at a high speed. Seizing the back of the chariot with one hand, he

brought both horses and driver to a halt. ... But in the end, as Homer says, those who glory in their strength are doomed to perish by it, and so Polydamas perished through his own might. He entered a cave together with his best friends to escape the summer heat. As bad luck would have it, the roof began to crack and it was obvious that the cave could not hold up much longer and would fall in quickly. Recognizing the disaster that was coming, the others turned and ran out; but Polydamas decided to stay. He held up his hands in the belief that he could prevent the cave from falling in and that he would not be crushed by the mountain. His end came here.

49   Pausanias VII.27.7   *ca.* A.D. 170

The people of Pellene will not even mention the name of Chairon who won twice in the Isthmian Games and four times in the Olympics (*356-344 B.C.*) in the wrestling. This is because he overthrew the constitution of Pellene and received from Alexander the Great the most invidious of all gifts—to be established as tyrant of one's own fatherland.

50   Athenaeus, *The Gastronomers* XI.509B   *ca.* A.D. 228

Some of the philosophers of the Academy today live wickedly and disgracefully. They are famous although they have gained fortunes by means of sacrilege and trickery; they remind me of Chairon of Pellene who attended the lectures of Plato and Xenokrates. He became the bitter tyrant of his city and not only drove out the best citizens of the city, but also gave their property to their slaves and forced their wives to marry their slaves. Such were the benefits which he derived from the beautiful *Republic* and the illegal *Laws*.

51   Diodorus Siculus XVII.100-101   *ca.* 30 B.C.

Alexander the Great held a huge banquet for his friends (*325 B.C.*). During the drinking something occurred which is worth mention. Among the companions of the king was a Macedonian named Koragos who was very strong in body and who had distinguished himself frequently in battle. The drink made him pugnacious, and he challenged to a duel one Dioxippos of Athens, an athlete who had won several glorious victories (*including one in the pankration at Olympia in 336 B.C.*). As might be expected of those in their cups, the guests egged them on and Dioxippos accepted the challenge. Alexander set the day for the battle, and when the time came for the duel thousands of men assembled for the spectacle. Because he was one of them, the Macedonians and Alexander rooted for Koragos, while the Greeks favored Dioxippos. Koragos came onto the field of honor clad in the finest armor, while the Athenian was naked with his body oiled and carrying a well-balanced club.

Both men were marvellous to see in their magnificent physical conditions and their desire for the fight. The spectators anticipated a veritable battle of gods. The Macedonian looked like Ares as he inspired terror through his stature and the brilliance of his weapons; Dioxippos resembled Herakles in his strength and athletic training, and even more so because he carried a club.

As they approached each other, the Macedonian hurled his javelin from the proper distance, but Dioxippos bent his body slightly and avoided it. Then the Macedonian poised his long pike and charged, but when he came within reach, the Greek struck the pike with his club and splintered it. Now Koragos was reduced to fighting with his club and splintered it. Now Koragos was reduced to fighting with his sword, but as he went to draw it, Dioxippos leaped upon him, grabbed his swordhand in his own left hand, and with his other hand he upset his opponent's balance and knocked his feet from under him. As Koragos fell to the ground, Dioxippos placed his foot on the other's neck and, holding his club in the air, looked to the crowd.

The spectators were in an uproar because the man's incredible skill and superiority. Alexander motioned for Koragos to be released, then broke up the gathering and left, clearly annoyed at the defeat of the Macedonian. Dioxippos released his fallen foe and left as winner of a resounding victory. His compatriots bedecked him with ribbons for the victory which he had won on behalf of all the Greeks. But Fortune did not permit him to boast of his victory for very long.

The king became increasingly antagonistic toward Dioxippos, and Alexander's friends and indeed all the Macedonians about the court, envious of Dioxippos' *arete,* persuaded one of the servants to hide a gold drinking cup under the pillow of his dining couch. During the next symposion they pretended to find the cup and accused him of theft. This placed Dioxippos in a shameful and disgraceful position. He understood that the Macedonians were in a conspiracy against him, and he got up and left the symposion. When he had returned to his own quarters, he wrote a note to Alexander about the trick which had been played on him, gave this to his servants for delivery to the king, and them committed suicide. He may have been ill-advised to accept the duel, but he was even more foolish to have done away with himself, for it gave his critics the chance to say that it was a real hardship to have great strength of body, but little of mind.

52   Aelian, *Var. Hist.* X.19   *ca.* A.D. 220
Eurydamas of Cyrene won the boxing, even though his opponent knocked out his teeth. To keep his opponent from having any satisfaction, he swallowed them.

53   *Anth. Pal.* XI.82
Charmos once ran the *dolichos* against five competitors, but came in seventh. You will probably ask, "Since there were six contestants, how could he come in seventh?" The reason was that a friend of his ran onto the track shouting "Go Charmos!" Thus he came in seventh, and if he had five more friends he would have finished twelfth.

54   *Anth. Pal.* XI.85
Once while running the *hoplitodromos,* Marcus was still running at midnight. The custodians mistook him for one of the honorary stone statues which line the track, and locked up the stadium. The next day they opened the stadium and found that Marcus had finished the first lap.

55   Athenaeus, *The Gastronomers* I.14F-15A   *ca.* A.D. 228
In this passage Athenaeus quotes from Antiphanes who was a comic
poet of the fourth century B.C., and from Juba of Mauretania who
wrote in the early first century after Christ.

The so-called *folliculus* was invented by Atticus of Naples, the
paidotribes, for the exercises of Pompey the Great. The game which
is called, on account of the ball, *harpastum* used to be called
phaininda. I like this game best of all.

Ball-games produce considerable exertion and fatigue, and severe
twistings of the neck. Thus Antiphanes says: "Ouch, what a pain in
the neck I've got." Antiphanes depicts the game of *phaininda* as
follows: "He caught the ball and laughed as he passed it to one
player at the same time as he dodged another. He knocked another
player out of the way, and picked one up and set him on his feet, and
all the while there were screams and shouts: 'Out of bounds!' 'Too
far!' 'Past him!' 'Over his head!' 'Under!' 'Over!' 'Short!' 'Back in
the huddle!'

The game was called *phaininda* either from the feinting of ball
players, or from the name of its inventor who was, according to Juba
of Mauretania, Phainestios the *paidotribes.*

56   Galen, *On Exercise with the Small Ball*   *ca.* A.D. 180
Galen began his career as an obscure gladiator and medical trainer,
but rose to become the court physician of the emperor Marcus
Aurelius. He does not hark back to an earlier period, but reflects the
practices of his own day. In these we can see a change to a more
scientific system of physical education which had evolved from the
teachings of generations of gymnasium trainers.

The most eminent philosophers and physicians of antiquity have
discussed adequately the benefits to health of gymnastic exercises
and diet, but no one has ever set forth the superiority of exercises
with the small ball. I am thus justified in setting forth my thoughts
on the subject.

I believe that the best of all exercises is the one which not only
exercises the body, but also refreshes the spirit. The men who
invented hunting were wise and well acquainted with the nature of
man, for they mixed its exertions with pleasure, delight, and rivalry.

Of course, there is a refreshment common to all exercises, but there are special advantages to the exercises with the small ball as I will now show.

First is its convenience. If you think of how much equipment and time is needed for hunting, you know that no politician or craftsman can participate in such sports, for they require a wealthy man with plenty of equipment and leisure time. But even the poorest man can play ball, for it requires no nets nor weapons nor horses nor hunting dogs, but only a ball and a small one at that. It does not interfere with a man's other pursuits and causes him to neglect none of them. And what could be more convenient than a game in which everyone, no matter his status or career, can participate?

You will also fine that it is the best all-around exercise if you stop to think about the possibilities and the natures of the other exercises. You will find that one is violent, another gentle; that one exercises the upper part of the body, or some part of the body such as the hips or the head or the hands or the chest, instead of the whole body. None keeps all the parts of the body equally in motion; none has a pace which can be speeded up and slowed down again. Only the exercise with the small ball achieves all this.

When the players line up on opposite sides and exert themselves to keep the one in the middle from getting the ball, then it is a violent exercise with many neck-holds mixed in with wrestling holds. Thus the head and the neck are exercised by the neck-holds, and the sides and chest and stomach are exercised by the hugs and shoves and tugs and the other wrestling holds. In this game the hips and legs are violently stretched and strained, for they provide a base for such exertion. The combination of running forward, backward, and jumping sideways is no small exercise for the legs; if the truth be told, this is the only exercise which puts all parts of the leg in motion. There is exertion on one set of tendons and muscles in running forward, upon another set in running backward, and upon yet another in jumping sideways. The man who moves his legs in only one motion, as for example the runner, exercises them irregularly and unevenly.

Just as ball playing is a good exercise for the legs, so it is even better for the arms, for it is customary to catch the ball in every sort of position. The variety of positions will strain different muscles to varying degrees at different times. You will also understand that ball playing trains the eye if you think about how the player will not catch the ball if he has not judged its flight accurately. The player will also sharpen his critical abilities by planning how to catch the ball and stay out of the middle, or how to snatch the ball if he happens to be in the middle. Thinking alone will keep weight down, but if it is mixed with some exercise and rivalry which ends in pleasure, it promotes health in the body and intelligence in the mind. This is an important benefit if an exercise can aid both the body and the mind toward the *arete* which is inherent in each.

You can easily understand that ball-playing trains for the two most important maneuvers which a state entrusts to its generals: to attack at the proper time and to defend the booty already amassed. There is no other exercise so suited to training in the guarding of gains, the retrieval of losses, and the foresight of the plan of the enemy. Most exercises produce the opposite effects by making the mind slow, sleepy, and dull. Even those who compete in the wrestling at the *stephanitic* games tend more toward fleshiness than toward the practice of *arete*; at least most of them have grown fat and have difficulty in breathing. Such men are of no use as generals in war or as administrators of imperial and civil businesss. It is better to give a job to pigs than to them.

You may think that I favor running and other weight reducing exercises. That is not so, for I condemn a lack of moderation in anything. Therefore I do not approve of running, for it reduces the weight too much and provides no training in courage. Victory in war does not belong to those who can run away the fastest, but to those who are able to prevail in close encounters. The Spartans did not become the most powerful because they could run the fastest, but because they had the courage to stand and fight. As far as health is concerned, any exercise is unhealthy in direct proportion to its unequal development of all parts of the body. Thus in running some parts of the body are overly exerted, while other parts are not exercised at all. This is not good, for it nourishes the seeds of disease and weakens strength.

I especially favor that exercise which promotes sufficient health for the body, harmonious development of its parts, and *arete* in the spirit. All of these are to be found in exercise with the small ball. It can benefit the mind in every way, and it exercises all the parts of the body equally. It thus contributes to health and to moderation in physical condition, for it causes neither excessive corpulence nor immoderate thinness. It is also suitable for actions which require strength and to those demanding speed. Thus the most strenuous form of ball-playing is in no way inferior to other exercises.

Let us consider its most gentle form. There are times when we need this form due to our age which is either not yet ready for severe exertion, or no longer able to exercise strenuously, or due to a desire for relaxation or for recuperation from an illness. I believe that in this form ball-playing is also superior to all the other exercises. No other exercise is so gentle if you wish to practice it gently. You need only to move in moderation at some times, and to stay put at others. Afterwards one should have a soft rubdown with oil and a hot bath. This is the most gentle of exercises, and it is thus beneficial for one who needs rest, for restoring ill health, and for old and young alike.

Moderate exercises between the extremes which I have already described can also be practiced with the small ball. One should be aware of this in order to take full advantage of the game. If, as happens to all of us, some necessary work has overtaxed some parts of the body, they can be rested while the parts which were idle can be exercised until the whole body has been equally exercised. Throwing from a distance and with vigor requires little or no exertion by the legs, and thus rests the lower part of the body while exercising the upper parts rather strenuously. Running swiftly over a large area while throwing only occasionally from a distance exercises the lower parts more than the upper. Quickness and speed in the game, without heavy exertion, exercise the lungs. Vigor in tackling, throwing, and catching, but without speed, stretch and strengthen the body. When vigor and speed are both present, both the body and the lungs will be exercised. The proper amount of stretching and relaxing cannot be written. This cannot be predicted, but must be learned for each individual by experience. Even the correct exercise is ruined if it is not used in the proper amounts. This should be the business of the *paidotribes* who is in charge of the exercises.

Let me now conclude this discussion. I do not want to omit from my list of the advantages of ball-playing that it does not have the dangers which most other exercises have. Sprinting has killed many men by rupturing important blood vessels. So too a loud and prolonged shouting has caused serious injuries to many men. Violent horseback riding has ruptured the kidneys and injured the chest and sometimes the testes. I do not even mention the stumblings of horses which have frequently thrown riders from their seats and killed them. So too the *halma* and the diskos and exercises in digging have

injured many. Do I even need to speak of wrestlers? They are all
lame or sprained or bruised or permanently disabled in some part of
their bodies. If, in addition to the advantages already discussed,
there is also present in ball-playing a freedom from danger, then this
must be the best exercise of all.

57   Pollux, *Names* IX.103-107   *ca.* A.D. 180
*Pollux, who was a rhetorician and held a Professorship at the
University of Athens, wrote a thesauros of terms and names.
Although his work survives to us only in the form of a ninth century
after Christ abridgement, even this abbreviated form contains much
of interest. The following passage is part of a section concerned with
the names of children's games.*

The names of children's ball-games were *episkyros, phaininda,
aporrhaxis, ourania. Episkyros* was also called *Ephebike* and
commonball. It was usually played with opposing teams of equal
number. In the middle a line was drawn with a chip of stone which
they called a *skyros.* They set the ball on tnis line, and each team
drew another line behind the opposition. The team which got the
ball first threw it over the opposition whose job it was to grab the ball
while it was still moving and throw it back the other way. This would
continue until one team had pushed the other over the back line.

Phaininda got its name either from its inventor, Phainindos, or
from the word for feinting, since the player fakes a throw to one
player, but actually throws to another, and thus deceives the player
who expected the ball. This resembles the game with the small ball
which is called *harpaston* from the word for snatching away. One
might call *phaininda* the game with the soft ball.

Aporrhaxis has the form of bouncing the ball vigorously on the
ground, and dribbling it again and again with the hand. The
number of bounces is counted.

Ourania is played with one player bending backward and
throwing the ball up into the sky. The others compete in snatching
the ball before it falls back to the ground. When they dribbled a ball
against a wall, they counted the number of bounces. The loser was
called the donkey and had to do whatever he was told. The winner
was called the king and gave the orders.

58   Vitruvius, *On Architecture* V.11   *ca* 30 B.C.

Vitruvius was a practicing architect whose treatise on architecture is the only one of many in antiquity which has survived. In this passage he described the layout of a Greek athletic complex, and his description corresponds very well to the third century B.C. palaestra-gymnasium buildings at Olympia.

Although the construction of a palaestra is not common in Italy, its plan has been handed down and it therefore seems worthwhile to explain the palaestra and to show how it is planned among the Greeks.

In palaestrai square or oblong peristyle courts are to be made with a perimeter of two *stadia,* a distance which the Greeks call *diaulos.* Three sides of the court are to be single colonnades; the fourth side is to be the one which faces south and it is to be a double colonnade so that, when there are rain storms with heavy winds, the rain will not reach the interior of the colonnade.

On the three sides of the court with single colonnades there are to be planned spacious *exedrai* with seats where philosophers, rhetoricians, and other who delight in studies can sit and discuss their subjects. In the double colonnade, however, the following elements are to be located: in the middle there is to be an *ephebeion* (this is an especially large *exedra* with seats) the length of which is to be one-third greater than its width. Next to this on the right as we face it is to be a *korykion.* Next after this room is to be a *konisterion,* and next to the *konisterion* at the corner of the colonnade is to be a cold bath which the Greeks call a *loutron.* To the left of the *ephebeion* is to be an *elaiothesion,* and next after the *elaiothesion* is to be the *frigidarium,* and from this room is to be the entrance to the furnace room at the corner of the colonnade. Next behind the furnace room toward the interior from the *frigidarium* is to be placed a vaulted sweating room with its length twice its width. Part of the space behind this room is to be for the *laconicum* and the other part, at the corner of the building, is to be for a warm bath. These are the arrangements within the palaestra.

Outside the palaestra three colonnades are to be arranged. One of these is to be entered from the peristyle of the palaestra. The other two colonnades are to have running tracks and be located to the left and to the right of the first colonnade. Of these colonnades, the one which faces north is to be double and especially wide; the others are to be single colonnades. Within these colonnades there are to be walkways at least ten feet wide along the back wall and along the columns. The central area is to be excavated down to a level track a foot and one-half below the walkways with steps down from the walkways to the track which is to be at least twelve feet wide. Thus the clothes of those on the walkways will not be stained by the oil of those who are exercising. This sort of colonnade is called a *xystos* by the Greeks whose athletes exercise during the winter in covered tracks a *stadion* in length. Next to the *xystos* and to the double colonnade are to be open-air walkways which the Greeks call *paradromides*. Here the athletes exercise even in the winter when the weather is good. The *xystoi* are to be laid out so that there are groves of plane trees between the two colonnades, and walkways are to be made of cement among the trees. Behind a *xystos* the stadium is to be planned so that large crowds can watch the athletes in comfort.

59   Antiphon, *Second Tetralogy* 2   *ca.* 425 B.C.

An Athenian youth has been killed in the gymnasium and another youth brought to trial for the homicide. This is one of the speeches prepared by Antiphon for the father of the accused boy to deliver to an Athenian court in the boy's defense. It reveals, in addition to some of the types of arguments which were used in the courts, some of the common practices in the gymnasium and, implicitly, a high degree of literacy in Athens.

It is now clear to me that misfortunes themselves and necessity can force those who dislike litigation into court, and those who are quiet to be loud and to say and do much which is contrary to their nature. I am not, nor do I want to be, the type of man who likes to appear in court, unless I have been fooling myself, but I have now been forced by misfortune to change my habits and appear as a defendant, and this in a case where I am hard pressed to understand the exact truth, and even more hard pressed to know how to present it to you. But I am forced by sheer necessity, gentlemen of the jury, and I must take refuge in your mercy.

I thought that, by educating my son in those subjects which especially benefit the state, both the state and I would be rewarded. The result has not been what I had thought it would be. The lad, not because of insolence or mischief, but because he was practicing the javelin with his mates in the gymnasium, did hit someone, but killed no one if the truth be known. He has been blamed for the mistake of another.

We would not be able to show that my son had not caused the boy's death had the javelin struck him outside the area marked for its flight. But the boy ran into the path of the javelin and thus put his body in its way. Hence my son was unable to hit that for which he had aimed, and the boy was hit because he ran under the javelin, and the cause of the accident which is attributed to us was not one of our own making. The running into the path was the cause of the boy being hit, and my son is unjustly accused. He did not hit anyone who stayed away from his target. Moreover, since it is clear to you that the other boy was not struck while standing still, but only after moving of his own volition into the path of the javelin, it should be quite clear to you that he was killed because of his own error. He would not have been killed had he remained still and not run across.

Now both sides in this trial are agreed that the boy's death was accidental, and the guilt of the death must belong to the one who was guilty of error. My son was guilty of no error. He was practicing not what had been forbidden, but what he had been instructed to do. He was not among those who were practicing other exercises when he threw the javelin, but among the other javelin throwers. He did not hit the other boy because he missed his target and threw into the bystanders. He did everything properly and as he had intended. Thus he was not the cause of an accident, but the victim of one, for he was prevented from hitting this target.

On the other hand, the dead boy wished to run forward, but missed the opportunity when he could have crossed without being hit. The result may not have been what he had intended, but he was guilty of an error which had an effect upon his own person. He paid the price of his mistake and has already received justice which causes us no joy, but rather sympathy and sorrow.

60   Aristotle, *The Constitution of the Athenians* 42   *ca.* 325 B.C.
We learn here something of the compulsory Ephebic training of every potential Athenian citizen. In addition to the clear connections beween athletics and this training which was a prerequisite of the good citizen, we may infer that there was no compulsory education

*beyond the Ephebic training. Aristotle expresses his opinions upon
this system elsewhere (see below, no. 62), but we can also infer,
although Aristotle does not explicitly state as much, that a basic
literacy for every Athenian citizen will have been assured during the
Ephebic training.*

Citizenship belongs to those whose parents were both citizens, and
they are registered in their *demes* when they are eighteen years old.
When they are about to be registered, the members of the *deme* vote
upon them. They vote first as to whether the candidates have been
shown to be of legal age. If not, the candidates are returned to the
boys. Secondly, they vote as to whether the candidate is a free man
and of legitimate birth. If they vote that he is not a free man, he
appeals to a court of law, and the members of the *deme* select five of
their members to argue the case against him. If the court decides
that he has no right to be registered in the *deme*, the city sells him
into slavery. After this the *Boule* examines those who have been
registered and if it finds anyone who is younger than eighteen, it
fines the members of the *deme* who registered him. When the
epheboi have been examined, their fathers meet in tribal divisions
and select the three men of forty years of age or more from each tribe
whom they think are the best and most suitable to be in charge of the
epheboi. From these thirty men the people elect by a show of hands
one from each of the ten tribes to be the *sophronistes*, and one from
all of the Athenians to be the *kosmetes* in charge of them all.

The *kosmetes* and the *sophronistai* then collect the *epheboi* and
first make a tour of the temples and shrines. They then go to
Peiraius and some of them garrison Mounichia and others Akte. The
people also elect by a show of hands two *paidotribai* and *didaskaloi*
for them who are to teach them infantry drills and the use of the
bow, the javelin, and the sling. The people give a *per diem* of $16 to
each of the *sophronistai* and a *per diem* of $10 to each of the
epheboi. The *sophronistes* of each tribe takes the pay of his *epheboi*
and buys their provisions in common, for each tribe eats together,
and he is in charge of all the other supplies as well. This is the way
that they spend the first year.

The following year there is an assembly in the theater and the
epheboi march in review for the people. They receive a shield and a
spear from the city, and they patrol the countryside and are
garrisoned in the border guard posts. They are on guard for two
years. They wear a *chlamys* and are completely tax exempt. They are

allowed to be neither plaintiff nor defendant in law suits in order that they have no excuse for absences. There are exceptions in the cases of estates, of exercising the right to claim an heiress by marriage, and of priesthoods which may have been inherited. When the two years have passed, they have become full citizens.

61   Plato, *Laws* 794D-796D   *ca.* 350 B.c.

In his ideal state Plato is much concerned with the education of the young. This education is to begin with the expectant mother keeping the fetus in a state of constant motion which is to continue until the child has reached the age of three. For the next three years the child is to be supervised in closely regulated play, and instruction proper is to begin at the age of six for boys and girls alike. This is to be under the supervision of elected officials of at least fifty years of age in three public gymnasia and exercise fields distributed around the city. The test of the validity of education is to be its service and utility to the state, and physical education plays a large role in the system as can be seen in the following.

It is a nearly universal and ignorant opinion that the right and the left hands are naturally different and adapted for different tasks. But the feet and legs are clearly equal to one another in abilities, and it is because of the stupidity of nurses and mothers that we have all become lame, so to speak, in our hands. For in natural ability the two limbs are equal, but we have made them different by constantly using them incorrectly. This makes no difference in trivial matters as, for example, whether a man uses the left hand for the fiddle and the right for the bow or vice-versa. But it is something like mindlessness to follow these examples and set habits when it is not necessary. This is shown by the Skythian custom of using both hands interchangeably for the functions of drawing the bow and of fitting the arrow to it. There are numerous similar examples which teach us that the left hand is no weaker by nature than the right, and that those who think so are wrong. This matters little in the case of the fiddle and other such instruments, as we have already said, but it matters very much when we come to use weapons, especially at close quarters. There is a vast difference here between the trained and the untrained, between the practiced and the unpracticed. Just as the athlete who is thoroughly trained in the *pankration* or boxing or

wrestling is capable of fighting with his left limbs and does not move
the left side as if it were numb or lame, so too with weapons of war
and everything else the man who possesses a pair of arms or a pair of
legs should use them all to equal advantage and allow none of them
to go untrained or without practice. Indeed, if a man had a hundred
hands, he should be able to throw a hundred missiles at once. These
matters must be the concern of the male and the female officers of
instruction. The women must oversee the feeding of the infants and
their games, and the men must oversee the lessons of the children, so
that all the boys and girls may be sound of hand and foot and may
not have their natural abilities lamed by their habits.

The lessons may be divided into two types: the gymnastic which
concern the body, and the musical which refresh the soul. There are
two kinds of gymnastic lessons: wrestling and dancing. There are
two types of dancing: the free and noble, and that which aims at
physical fitness, agility, and beauty by exercising the various parts of
the body and by bestowing a rhythmical motion. The lessons in
upright wrestling, with their disentangling of necks and hands and
sides of the body, when practiced with vigor and a graceful firmness
and toward the end of strength and health, must not be omitted
since these lessons are useful for all purposes.

When we reach this point in our legislation we should charge both
the pupils and their teachers that the latter should impart these
lessons gently, and the former receive them gratefully.

62   Aristotle, *Politics* 1337a-1339a   *ca.* 325 B.C.
Aristotle, like Plato, considers the question of utility as a primary
test of education, but his system is at once both more pragmatic and
more idealistic than Plato's. As he discusses contemporary theories
and practices, and argues for his system, Aristotle raises basic
questions about education, and many of them are familar today.

No one would disagree that the lawgiver should give special
attention to the education of the young. Inasmuch as there is one
end for the whole state, it is clear that education must also be one
and the same for all and that the supervision of this must be public
and not private in the way that each man now supervises the
education of his own children, teaching them whatever he thinks

they should be taught. There ought to be public supervision for matters of public concern. At the same time one ought to think not that a citizen belongs to himself, but that all citizens belong to the state, for each is a part of the state, and the supervision of each part ought naturally to have regard for the supervision of the whole. One might praise the Spartans in this respect, for they pay great attention to the education of their children and conduct it on a public system.

It is clear that there ought to be legislation about education, and that education ought to be conducted on a public system. But one must not forget what the nature of education is, and what ought to be taught. At present there are disagreements about these questions. Not everyone agrees about what the young ought to learn and whether the goal should be *arete* or the good life, nor is it clear whether studies should be directed toward the development of intellect or of character. Troublesome questions arise from the current status of education, and it is not clear whether the student ought to study those things which are useful for life, or those which lead toward *arete,* or those which are theoretical. Each of these has its supporters. Nor is there even agreement about which studies lead toward *arete.* This starts from a disagreement about what constitutes *arete* which leads logically to a disagreement about training for *arete.*

It is at least clear that the young must be taught those utilitarian things which are absolutely necessary, but not everything which is utilitarian. A distinction must be made between those pursuits which are liberal and those which are not liberal; that is, the student ought not to participate in those utilitarian pursuits which lead to vulgarity. It is necessary to define as vulgar any pursuit or craft or science which renders useless the body or soul or mind of free men for the practice of *arete.* Thus we call vulgar those crafts which deteriorate the condition of the body and those employments which earn wages, for they make the mind preoccupied and degraded. Even liberal sciences are liberal only up to a point, for to devote oneself to them too rigorously and completely can have the damaging results of vulgarity. The purpose of one's pursuits or studies also makes a great difference. If the purpose is for the inherent joy of the project, or for friendship, or for *arete,* it is not illiberal. He who does the very same thing, however, because of other people would seem to be acting as a servant or a slave.

There are essentially four areas of normal education: reading and writing, physical exercises, music, and the fourth, according to some people, drawing. Reading and writing and drawing are important because they are useful in life and serviceable. Physical education is important because it contributes to manliness. But someone might question music. This is because, at present, most participate in it for the sake of pleasure. But those who include music in education from the beginning do so, as has often been said, because nature itself seeks not only to work properly, but also to relax nobly. For if both work and leisure are necessary, but leisure is more desirable as a goal than work, then one ought to ask what is the proper occupation of leisure. Certainly leisure must not be spent in playing, for it would necessarily follow that play is the goal of life. Since play ought not to occupy times of leisure, but rather times of work (for play gives rest, and the weary need rest, and work is accomplished by weariness), it follows that we must use play at the proper times since we are using play as a therapy due to its relaxation of the soul and its restfullness because of its pleasure. Leisure, on the other hand, seems to contain pleasure and happiness and the good life, and this belongs not to those who are working, but to those at leisure. The man who is working works for some goal which he does not possess, but happiness is a goal already reached. Hence it is clear that some subjects are to be learned and studied simply for the pleasure in the pursuit of them, and that these studies and lessons are goals in themselves, while those branches of learning which relate to work are to be learned and studied as means to some other ends. For this reason our predecessors included music in education not as a necessity (for there is nothing necessary about it), nor as utilitarian in the way that reading and writing are useful for business and personal finances and learning and politics nor in the way that drawing is useful in making one a better judge of the works of craftsmen nor in the way that physical education helps with health and strength (for we do not see such results from music). Music therefore remains as a leisure pursuit which is a form of pastime appropriate to free men.

It is therefore clear that there is an aspect of education which ought to be taught to our sons not because it is useful or necessary, but because it frees the spirit and enobles the soul. It is also clear that some of the useful things ought to be studied by the young not only because of their utility, such as reading and writing, but also because they can lead to the study of other things. In the same way drawing shoul. be studied, not so that one might not be cheated in buying and selling equipment, but rather because this study makes a man observant of beauty. To seek utility in everything is not appropriate to men who are of great spirit and free.

Since it is clear that education by habit must precede education by reason, and that education of the body must precede education of the mind, it is also clear that the children must be turned over to the *gymnastai* and the *paidotribai,* for the one works with the condition of the body, the other with its actions.

At the present time some of the states with the greatest reputation for attention to their children produce in them such an athletic condition as to detract from the form and growth of the body. The Spartans, although they have avoided this mistake, turn their children into little animals through their labors which they think contribute to manliness. But, as has often been said, attention must be paid not just to one virtue, nor even to one virtue before all others. Indeed, they do not even consider whether their training leads to that virtue. For we see in the cases of animals and of foreign races that courage and manliness do not belong to the wildest, but rather to the more gentle and lion-like temperaments. There are many foreign races inclined toward murder and cannibalism which have no share in manly courage. Nobility and not animalism should play the leading role, for neither a wolf nor any other animal will risk a noble danger, but only a good man. Those who train their children in athletics to the exclusion of other necessities make their children truly vulgar and available to the state for only one kind of work, and actually train them worse for this one job than others do.

It is, then, agreed that we should make use of physical education and how we should make use of it. Until puberty lighter exercises should be applied, and forced diets and required works forbidden in order that there be no impediment to growth. There is no small proof that such training can stunt growth. In the list of Olympic victors one can find only two or three who have won in both the boys' category and the men's category. The strength of those who train too hard in youth is robbed by the required exercises. When the boys have spent three years after puberty on other lessons, then it is proper that the next period of their lives be spent on exercises with the required diets.

63   Suetonius, *Julius Caesar* 39   45 B.C.

Suetonius, who published his biographies of the first twelve Emperors in ca. A.D. 120, here tells us of the triumphal "games" put on by Caesar. From them we gain an idea of the status and importance of athletics in Roman society.

Caesar's public spectacles were of various kinds. They included a gladiatorial combat, stage-plays in every quarter of Rome performed in every language, chariot races in the Circus, athletic competitions, and a mock naval battle. I shall give more detail of these spectacles.

At the gladiatorial combat in the Forum Furius Leptinus, a man of praetorial family, fought Quintus Calpenus, a former senator and lawyer, to the death. The sons of petty kings from Asia and Bithynia performed a Pyrrhic sword dance.

One of the plays was written and performed by Decimus Laberius, a Roman knight, who thus forfeited his rank. But after the performance he was given a large sum of money and had his gold ring, the badge of knighthood, restored to him. The track in the Circus was lengthened for the races and a ditch dug around it, and young noblemen competed in driving four-horse and two-horse chariots, and rode pairs of horses jumping from one to the other. The so-called Troy Game, a mock battle introduced by Aeneas, was performed by two troops of boys, one older and the other younger.

Wild beast battles took place for five consecutive days and finally there was a battle between two armies, each made up of 500 infantry soldiers, twenty elephants, and thirty cavalry. To make room for this, the *metae* where the chariots turned in the Circus were removed and the two camps pitched in their places facing one another.

The athletic competitions were held in a temporary stadium built for the purpose in the Campus Martius and lasted for three days.

The naval battle was fought on an artificial lake dug in the lesser Codeta, between heavily manned Tyrian and Egyptian ships with two, three, and four banks of oars. Such a mob thronged to all these spectacles from all directions that many strangers had to stay in tents pitched among the roads and streets, and the press of the crowd was often such that many were crushed to death. The victims included two senators.

64   Dio Chrysostom XXVIII.5-8   ca. A.D. 74
See above, no. 33.

Melancomas of Caria was the most courageous and the biggest of all mankind, and the most beautiful. Had he remained a private citizen and not practiced boxing at all, I believe that he still would have become widely known simply for his beauty. Even so all heads, even of those who did not know who he was, turned wherever he went. And yet he dressed in such a way as to escape rather than attract attention. No matter the number of boys, no matter the number of men who were exercising, when he stripped no one looked at anyone else. And although beauty customarily leads to softness, even for one who is only moderately beautiful, Melancomas was the most moderate of men despite his beauty. And though he despised his beauty, he preserved it none the less and despite his rough sport. For though he was a boxer, he was as whole as a runner. He trained so rigorously and so far exceeded others in exercising that he could remain for two whole days in succession with his hands up, and no one ever saw him drop his guard and rest as is customary with others. Thus he could force his opponents to give up, not only before he had received a blow, but even before he had landed one on them. He did not consider striking or receiving a blow a sign of manliness, but as a sign of a lack of stamina and of willpower. He thought it a noble achievement to last out the time without being beaten by the weight of his arms, without getting out of breath, and without being distressed by the heat.

It was for this reason that, from the time he began to compete at the Pythian Games, Melancomas was the first man in our knowledge to remain undefeated while winning the largest number and the most prestigious of crowns and defeating opponents neither feeble nor few. He surpassed his own father while still a youth, for he, the famous Melancomas of Caria who won many crowns including one at Olympia, did not remain undefeated.

Despite his splendid athletic achievements, Melancomas came to a pitiful end without having experienced any of the pleasures of life. Moreover, he was so ambitious that as he was dying he asked his boyhood friend, Athenodoros the pankratiast, how many days were left in the competition.

65 Suetonius, *Nero* 22-24   A.D.67
Although athletics continued in the Greek world under the Roman Empire, they were, like everything else, subject to Roman whim as is

shown most strikingly by this account of Nero's visit to Greece during which he "won" no fewer than 1808 crowns of victory at various festivals.

Soon Nero set his heart on driving a chariot himself and in a regular race. So, after a preliminary trial in the palace garden before an audience of slaves and loafers, he made his public debut at the Circus. For this occasion one of his freedmen replaced the official who dropped the flag to signal the start.

However, these incursions into the arts at Rome did not satisfy him for long, and he soon headed for Greece. His main reason stemmed from the fact that the Greek cities which sponsored regular music contests had adopted the policy of sending to him every prize for kithara-playing. He always accepted these prizes with great pleasure, giving the representatives of those cities the earliest audience of the day and invitations to private dinners. When the meal was over, they would beg Nero to sing and then applaud his performance resoundingly. This led him to say: "Only the Greeks are worthy of my genius, for they really listen to music." So he sailed off to Greece and, having landed, made the rounds of all the festivals.

Most contests were held only at long intervals, but he ordered them all to be held during his visit even if it meant repeating them after an irregular interval. He broke tradition at Olympia by the introduction of a music contest in the athletic games. When his freedman-secretary Halius reminded him that he was needed urgently at Rome, he would not be distracted but answered: "Yes, you have made yourself quite clear and I understand that you want me to return home. You would do better, however, by encouraging me to stay until I have proved myself worthy of my reputation."

No one was allowed to leave the theater during his performances, however urgent the reason, and the gates were kept locked. There are stories of women in the audience giving birth, and of men being so bored that they would sneak out by jumping off the wall at the back of the theater, or by playing dead and being carried away for burial. Nero's stage fright, his general nervousness, his jealousy of rivals, and his awe of the judges were more easily seen than believed. Although he was usually gracious and charming to the other competitors, whom he treated as equals, he would abuse them behind their backs and sometimes insulted them to their faces. He would bribe singers who were obviously very talented to sing off-key.

He would address the judges with extreme deference and say that he had done what he could and that the outcome was now in the hands of fortune but that, since they were men of reason and experience, they would know how to remove the element of luck. When they told him not to worry he would feel a little better, but still anxious, and he mistook the silence of some for harshness, and the embarrassment of others for distaste, and admitted that he regarded every one of them with suspicion.

He observed the rules very carefully, never daring to clear his throat and even using his forearm, instead of a handkerchief to wipe the sweat from his forehead. Once, while acting in a tragedy, he dropped his scepter and quickly picked it up, but was terrified of being disqualified. The accompanist who played the flute and served as prompter for his lines swore that the slip had not been noticed because the audience was listening and enraptured; and so he took heart again. Nero insisted upon announcing his own victories and this led him to enter the competitions for heralds. In order that he might destroy every trace of previous winners in his contests, he ordered that all their statues were to be pulled down, dragged away, and dumped into public latrines.

He took part in the chariot racing on several occasions, and at Olympia he drove a ten-horse team, a novelty which had been added to the festival just for him. However, he lost his balance and fell out of the chariot and had to be helped into it again. Nonetheless, even though he did not run the whole race and quit before the finish, the judges awarded him the crown of victory. On the eve of his departure for Rome, he presented the whole province where Olympia is located with its freedom, and granted Roman citizenship as well as large cash rewards upon the judges.

66   *Hesperia* 33 (1964), p. 320   *ca.* 565 B.C.
The inscription upon the base of a statue found at Nemea speaks to us as if from the statue itself.
   Aristis dedicated me to Zeus Kronios the King since he won the pankration at Nemea four times. Aristis is the son of Pheidon from Kleonai.

67   *IG XIV*, 747   A.D. 107

*The following inscription was discovered at Naples, and it sets forth
the career of an athlete of the first century after Christ. It tells us of
the existence of athletic guilds or unions, of the principal games of
the period, and something of their relative importance based upon
the order in which they are listed. It also indicates, especially when
contrasted with no. 66 above, a considerable change in athletics and
athletes in the more than 650 years between the two documents.*

To Good Fortune. The loyal and patriotic and reverent and itinerant
synodos of the Alexandrians honor Titus Flavius Archibius of
Alexandria, high priest for life of the entire *xystos*, victor incompar-
able, who won the *pankration* in the men's category at the 220th and
221st Olympiads (*A.D. 101 and 105*). In Rome at the third celebration of the Great Capitoline Games (*A.D. 94*) he won the *pankration*
in the *ageneios* category, and at their fourth celebration (*A.D. 98*) he
won the *pankration* in the men's category, and at their fifth celebration [*A.D. 102*) he won the *pankration* in the men's category, and
at their sixth celebration (*A.D. 106*) he again won the *pankration* in
the men's category, the first of mankind to do so. At the Heraklean
Victory Games held by the Emperor Nerva Trajan Caesar Augustus
Germanicus Dacicus he was crowned in the *pankration* in the men's
category. At the Pythian Games he won the *pankration* in the
ageneios category, and at the next Pythiad he won both the wrestling
and the *pankration* in the men's category, and at the next Pythiad he
won the *pankration* in the men's category, the first of mankind to do
so. At the Nemean Games ne won the *pankration* in the boys'
category and the *pankration* in the men's category three times in a
row, the first of mankind to do so. At the Isthmian Games he won
the *pankration* in the men's category. At the Aktian Games he won
the wrestling and the *pankration* in the *ageneios* category, and at the
next festival he won the pankration in the men's category, the first of
mankind to do so. At Naples he won the *pankration* in the *ageneios*
category and in the next two festivals he won the *pankration* in the
men's category. At the [*broken away*] he won the wrestling and the
pankration in the *ageneios* category, and at the next two festivals he
won the wrestling and the *pankration* in the men's category, and at
the next festival he won the *pankration* in the men's category, the
first of mankind to do so. At the Balbilleia Games at Ephesos he won
the wrestling and the boxing and the *pankration* in the men's
category, the first of mankind to do so. At the sacred four-year

games at Antioch he won the *pankration* in the boys' category and at
the next festival four years later he won the wrestling and the boxing
in the *ageneios* category, and at the next festival he won the
pankration in the men's category, and at the next festival again he
won the *pankration* in the men's category, the first of mankind to do
so. At the League of Asia Games at Smyrna he won the wrestling and
the *pankration* in the *ageneios* category. At the sacred four-year
games at Alexandria he won the *pankration* in the *ageneios* category
and four years later he won the *pankration* in the men's category and
again at the next festival he won the pankration in the men's
category and at the next festival he won the wrestling and the
pankration in the men's category, the first of mankind to do so. He
also has victories in wrestling and the pankration at the Shield of
Argos Games and many other four-year games in the boys',
ageneios, and men's categories.

68   Pliny the Younger, *Letters* **X.39, 40, 118, 119   A.D. 111**
These are some of the letters between Pliny, an Imperial representa-
tive in northern Asia Minor, and the Emperor Trajan. They reveal a
high degree of organization within the Roman administration of the
provinces, something of the conflict between the Roman dislike for
athletics and the Greek world's continued interest in athletics, and
something of the security felt by the athletes, probably because of
their unions, in daring to negotiate with the Emperor.

(Pliny to Trajan): The citizens of Nicaea, Sir, had their gymnasium burn down before my arrival. They have begun to rebuild it on
a larger scale than it was before, and have voted funds for the purpose which are in danger of being wasted. The structure is poorly
planned and unorganized. Furthermore, the present architect (who
is, to be sure, a rival of the architect who began the work) says that
the walls, even though they are twenty-two feet thick, cannot support
the load placed on them, because they are rubble at the core and
have no brick facing.

(Trajan to Pliny): Those little Greeks have a weakness for gymnasia. Perhaps, therefore, the citizens of Nicaea were overly ambitious in undertaking the construction of their gymnasium. But they
will have to be content with one which is just adequate for their
needs.

(Pliny to Trajan): Sir, the athletes are constantly complaining that they ought to receive the *obsonia* which you have established for the *iselastic* games from the day when they were crowned. They maintain that it is relevant not when they may be led triumphantly into their native city, but when they actually won the contest which is the cause of the *obsonia*. Since I am to countersign the *obsonia* payments with the notation *"iselastic* account," it is my strong inclination to believe that only the date when they have made their *iselasis* is to be considered.

The athletes are also asking for the *obsonia* for victories in the games which you have designated *iselastic* even though their victories at those games came before your designation. They maintain that this is only reasonable since the *obsonia* have been stopped for their victories at games which have been dropped from the *iselastic* list even though their victories at those games came while those games were still on the list. I seriously question whether such retroactive rewards are to be given, and I therefore beg that you instruct me upon the intention of your benefactions.

(Trajan to Pliny); I do not think that anything is owed the victor in an *iselastic* contest until the victor has made the *iselasis* into his own city. No retroactive *obsonia* are owed to the athletes who wor victories at the games which I have been pleased to place on the *iselastic* list if the victories antedate the games becoming *iselastic*. It is no argument that they have ceased to receive the *obsonia* for their victories in games which I have removed from the *iselastic* list. Although the status of those contests was changed, I did not demand that they refund what they had already received.

69   Philostratos, *On Gymnastics* 45   *ca.* A.D. 230
The general situation as well as the specific incident described below seem to be from Philostratos' own day, but the situation had clearly been developing over an extended period of time.

Such a luxurious life style as I have just described led to illegal practices among the athletes for the sake of money. I refer to the selling and buying of victories. I suppose that some surrender their chance at fame because of great destitution, but others buy a victory which involves no effort for the luxury which it promises. There are laws against temple robbers who mutilate or destroy a silver or gold dedication to the gods, but the crown of Apollo or of Poseidon, for which even the gods once competed, they are free to buy and free to sell. Only the olive at Elis still remains inviolate in accordance with its ancient glory. Let me give one of many possible examples which will illustrate what happens at the other games. A boy won the wrestling at Isthmia by promising to pay $24,000 to his opponent. When they went into the gymnasium on the next day, the loser demanded his money, but the winner said that he owed nothing since the other had tried after all to win. Since their differences were not resolved, they had recourse to an oath and went into the sanctuary at Isthmia. The loser then swore in public that he had sold Poseidon's contest, and that they had agreed upon a price of $24,000. Moreover, he stated this in a clear voice with no trace of embarrassment. The fact that this was told in front of witnesses may make it more truthful, but also all the more sacrilegious and infamous; he swore such an oath at Isthmia before the eyes of Greece. What disgrace might not be happening at the games in Ionia and Asia?

I do not absolve the *gymnastai* of blame for this corruption. They come to do their training with pockets full of money which they loan to the athletes at interest rates which are higher than business men who hazard sea trade have to pay. They care nothing for the reputations of the athletes, but give advice about the sale or purchase of a victory. They are constantly on the lookout for their own gain, either by making loans to those who are buying a victory, or by cutting off the training of those who are selling. I call these *gymnastai* peddlers, for they put their own interests first and peddle the *arete* of their athletes.

70   Galen, *Exhortation for Medicine* 9-14   *ca.* A.D. 180
Galen (see above, no 56) here attacks professional athletics, but his attack may be founded in a long-standing feud between physicians and trainers. In other words, he may well be more disturbed by the training practices of his day than by professionalism, but the two were inseparable. The Hippokrates whom Galen quotes was a Greek physician who died in 399 B.C.

Come now, my boys. You who have heard what I have said to this point must push ahead with the learning of an art so that some cheat or faker will not ever teach you some useless or evil art. Thus will you recognize that those pursuits are not arts which do not have the improvement of life as their goal. Of course, you understand most of those things which are not arts such as tumbling and walking a tight rope and spinning in a circle without becoming dizzy. I am suspicious only of the pursuit of athletics which might trick some youth into thinking that it is an art because it promises strength of body and reputation among the masses and a grant of money each day from the public treasury. Therefore it is best that we give this some forethought, for a person is not so easily deceived in a matter which he has already thought out.

The race of men has in common with the gods the gift of speech and in common with dumb animals the gift of life. It is convenient in education to pay attention to the perceptible advantages of communication, for if we have this we have the greatest of goods, but lacking this we are no better than dumb animals. Now the athletic training of the body lacks this and cannot, furthermore, gain even an equal footing with the dumb animals. For who is stronger than the lions or the elephants, and who can run faster than the hare? Who does not see that we thank the gods for nothing so much as the gift of the arts, and that the best of men are honored, not because they ran beautifully in the games or threw the diskos or wrestled, but because of their accomplishments and benefactions in the arts? Thus Asklepios and Dionysos were both men who became gods and worthy of the greatest honors, one because he gave us medicine and the other because he taught us the art of viticulture. If you do not want to believe me, then at least respect Pythian Apollo who said that Socrates was the wisest of all men.

All natural blessings are either mental or physical, and there is no other category of blessing. Now it is abundantly clear to everyone that athletes have never even dreamed of mental blessings. To begin with, they are so deficient in reasoning powers that they do not even know if they have a brain. Always gorging themselves on flesh and blood they keep their brains soaked in so much filth that they are unable to think accurately and are as mindless as dumb animals.

Perhaps it would be claimed that athletes achieve some of the physical blessings. Will they claim the most important blessing of all—health? You will find no one in a more treacherous physical condition if we are to believe Hippokrates who said that the extreme good health for which they strive is treacherous. And Hippokrates said something else which is liked by all: "Healthy training is moderation in diet, stamina in work." For he proposed for a program in health: "Work, food, drink, sleep, love, and all in moderation." But athletes overexert every day at their exercises, and they force-feed themselves, frequently extending their meals until midnight.

Thus too their sleep is immoderate. When normal people have ended their work and are hungry, the athletes are just getting up from their naps. In fact, their lives are just like those of pigs, except that pigs do not overexert nor force-feed themselves.

In addition to what I have already quoted, Hippokrates also said: "Excessive and sudden filling or emptying or heating or chilling or otherwise moving the body is dangerous." And he also said: "Excess is the enemy of nature." But athletes pay no attention to these or others of his wonderful sayings which they transgress, and their practices are in direct opposition to his doctrines of good health. Furthermore, the extreme conditioning of athletes is treacherous and variable, for there is no room for improvement and it cannot remain constant, and so the only way which remains is down hill. Thus their bodies are in good shape while they are competing, but as soon as they retire from competition degeneration sets in. Some soon die, some live longer but do not reach old age.

Since we have now considered the greatest of physical blessings, health, let us go on to the physical blessings which remain. With respect to beauty it is clear that natural beauty is not improved a bit for athletes, but that many athletes with well proportioned limbs are made exceedingly fat by the *gymnastai* who take them and stuff them with blood and flesh. Indeed, the faces of some are beat up and ugly, especially of those who have practiced the pankration or boxing. When their legs are finally broken or twisted permanently out of shape or their eyes gouged out I suppose that then especially is the beauty resulting from their way of life most clearly to be seen! While they are healthy this is the beauty which it is their good fortune to possess, but when they retire the rest of their bodies go to pot and their already twisted limbs are the cause of real deformities.

But perhaps they will claim none of the blessings which I h e mentioned so far, but will say that they have strength, indeed, that they are the strongest of men. But, in the name of the gods, what kind of strength is this and good for what? Can they do agricultural work such as digging or harvesting or plowing? But perhaps their strength is good for warfare? Euripides will tell us, for he said (*no. 79 below*): "Do men fight battles with diskoi in their hands?" Are they strong in the face of cold and heat? Are they rivals of Herakles so that they too, summer and winter, go barefoot clad in a skin and camp out to sleep under the heavens? In all these respects they are weaker than newborn babies.

I think that it has become abundantly clear that the practice of athletics has no use in the real business of life. You would further learn that there is nothing worth mention in such practice if I tell you that myth which some talented man put into words. It goes like this: if Zeus had it in mind that all the animals should live in harmony and partnership so that the herald was to invite to Olympia not only men but also animals to compete in the stadium, I think that no man would be crowned. In the *dolichos* the horse will be the best, the *stadion* will belong to the hare, and the gazelle will be first in the *diaulos*. Wretched men, nimble experts, none of you would be counted in the foot races. Nor would any of you descendants of Herakles be stronger than the elephant or the lion. I think that the bull will be crowned in the boxing, and that the donkey will, if he decides to, win the kicking crown. And so it shall be written in the history of these wide-open games that an ass beat the men in the *pankration:* "In the 21st Olympiad which was won by Brayer."

This myth shows quite nicely that athletic strength does not reside in human training. And yet, if athletes cannot be better than animals in strength, what other blessing do they share in?

Perhaps someone would say that they have a blessing in the pleasure of their bodies. But how can they derive any pleasure from their bodies if, during their athletic years they are in constant pain and suffering, and not only because of their exercises but also because of their forced feedings? And even when they have reached the age of retirement, their bodies are essentially if not completely crippled.

Are athletes perhaps to be worshipped like kings because they have large incomes? And yet they are all in debt, not only during the time when they are competing, but also after retirement. You will not find a single athlete who is wealthier than any business agent of a rich man. Furthermore, the most important aspect of a profession is not whether you can get rich at it, but whether you can always make a living from it. I refer to a stability of income which does not exist even for the managers of rich men, nor for tax collectors, nor for merchants. Finally, athletes have big incomes while they are actively competing, but when they retire money quickly becomes a problem for them and they soon run through their funds until they have less than they started with before their careers. Does any one loan them money without property for security?

Therefore, if any of you wants to prepare to make money safely and honestly, you must train for a profession which can be continued throughout life.

71   Herodotus III.129-133   519 B.C.
Demokedes, previously court physician to Polykrates the tyrant of Samos, has been captured by the Persians. Darius the Persian King is unaware of the existence of Demokedes until there is an accident.

One day Darius was out hunting and twisted his ankle as he dismounted from his horse. It was a severe sprain for the ankle had been completely dislocated. Darius had kept in attendance for some time some Egyptian doctors who had reputations for being the best of their profession, and he now summoned them. They, however, by their twisting and straining only made the foot worse. For seven days and nights Darius continued in such pain that he could not sleep. On the eighth day he was informed about the skill of Demokedes of Kroton by people who had seen him at work elsewhere. Darius ordered that he be brought forward immediately. He was brought as they found him among the slaves, dragging his chains and dressed in rags. They stood him in front of the throne and Darius asked him if he knew the art of medicine. Demokedes replied that he knew nothing of it, for he was afraid that he would never be allowed to return to Greece if he acknowledged his own skill. Darius, however, was not deceived and realized that Demokedes was concealing his skill. He therefore ordered the men who had brought Demokedes to fetch the whips and the iron spikes. With this Demokedes changed his tune and said that, although he did not understand very much, he had lived with a doctor for a time and had learned a bit about medicine. Despite this statement, Darius entrusted himself to Demokedes, and the latter, by using Greek remedies which were milder than those of his predecessors, enabled Darius to get some sleep and soon restored him to complete health. Darius, who had never expected to be able to use his foot again, presented Demokedes with two sets of gold chains which prompted Demokedes to ask if the reward for his cure was an enrichment of his slavery. Darius was amused by this and sent Demokedes off to his wives.

When the eunuchs had conducted him to the wives, they introduced him as the man who had saved the King's life. Thereupon the wives each scooped a cupful of gold from a chest and gave it to Demokedes. There was so much money that a servant by the name of Skiton collected a fortune simply from what spilled over.

The history of Demokedes was that he left his native Kroton in order to escape the harsh treatment of his father. He went first to Aigina where, within the first year, he surpassed the other doctors even though he was untrained and had no medical equipment or instruments. In the second year, the people of Aigina paid him a salary of $48,000. The next year the Athenians hired him away with a salary of $80,000, and the year after that Polykrates offered him $96,000. He accepted this and so went to Samos where the Persians captured him. It was largely because of Demokedes that Krotoniate doctors came to have such a high reputation.

After his cure of Darius, Demokedes lived in a big house in Susa, took his meals with the King, and had every privilege but the one of returning to Greece. The Egyptian doctors who had first treated Darius were going to be impaled, but were released as a result of Demokedes' intervention with Darius on their behalf. In fact, Demokedes' influence with the King was such that he was also able to secure the release of a professional soothsayer from Elis who had been with Polykrates and was lying in a wretched state with the slaves.

After a short time, something else happened. An abscess developed on the breast of Atossa the daughter of Cyrus and a wife of Darius. After a time, the abscess burst and began to spread the infection. At first, while it was still small, she hid it out of shame and told no one about it; but when it grew worse, she sent for Demokedes and showed it to him. He said that he would cure her if she would promise to do for him in return whatever he might ask of her. He stipulated that he would ask for nothing which would cause her shame, and upon these terms he treated and cured her.

As her part of the bargain, Atossa convinces Darius to send Demokedes out with a Persian mission to spy upon the defenses of Greece as a preliminary to a Persian invasion. When the mission finally comes to southern Italy, Demokedes jumps ship and finds his way back to Kroton. His erstwhile Persian companions pursue him, but the Krotoniates (after some debate) refuse to give him up.

The Persians returned to Asia and made no further attempt to scout out the coasts of Greece since they had lost their guide. Just before they left Kroton Demokedes told them to inform Darius that he was engaged to be married to the daughter of Milo the wrestler whose name was held in high esteem by the King. I think that Demokedes decided to make this marriage even though it cost him a large sum of money in order to show Darius that he was important in his own homeland.

72   Thucydides VI.16.2   415 B.C.

During the public debate which resulted in the decision to mount an Athenian invasion of Sicily, Alcibiades presented his case for being put in command of the expedition. A part of his argument is the following which shows something of the private wealth which was expended by competitors at the panhellenic games.

I think, Athenians, that I am worthy of the command. First of all, my deeds, which make me the object of public outcry, actually bring glory not only to my ancestors and myself, but also to my country, and this glory is mixed with practical advantage as well. The Greeks who had been hoping that our city was exhausted by the war came to think of our power as even greater than it is because of my magnificent *theoria* at Olympia. I entered seven four-horse chariots, a number never before entered by a private citizen, and I came in first, second, and fourth, and I provided all the trappings worthy of such a victory. For it is the custom that such accomplishments convey honor, and at the same time power is inferred from the achievement.

73   *Bull. Epig.* 1967, p. 569, no. 697   *ca.* 600 B.C.

The following brief and difficult inscription was discovered on a bronze tablet at Sybaris in southern Italy. It raises a fundamental question: how could Kleombrotos dedicate a tithe of his victory prize from the Olympic Games? What is a tenth of a crown of olive leaves? Do we have to do here, at this early date, with a monetary prize awarded to Kleombrotos by his home town in recognition of his Olympic victory?
See further below, no 74.

A gift. Kleombrotos son of Dexilaos having won at Olympia and having promised the prize to Athena, dedicated a tithe.

74   *IG* I² 77.11-17   *ca.* 430 B.C.
This decree of the Athenian people shows that, at least by the middle of the fifth century B.C. if not earlier, it was common for a city-state to reward her athletes who had been victorious at one of the panhellenic games with a prize worth something more than the simple crown awarded at the games themselves.

Those citizens who have won the athletic competitions at Olympia or Delphi or Isthmia or Nemea shall have a free meal every day for the rest of their lives in the *prytaneion* and other honors as well. Also those citizens who have won the *tethrippon* or the *keles* at Olympia or Delphi or Isthmia or Nemea shall have a free meal every day for the rest of their lives in the *prytaneion*.

75   Pausanias VI.13.1   *ca.*A.D. 170
The statue of Astylos of Kroton is the work of Pythagoras. Astylos won both the *stadion* and the *diaulos* in three successive Olympiads (*488, 484, 480 B.C.*). Because on the two latter occasions he announced that he was a Syracusan in order to please Hieron the son of Deinomenes and king of Syracuse, the citizens of Kroton pulled down his statue and turned his house into a prison.

76   Pausanias VI.2.6   *ca.* A.D. 170
There stands a statue of Antipater son of Kleinopater of Miletus who won the boxing in the boys' category (*388 B.C.*). Men from Syracuse, sent by the tyrant Dionysios to make a sacrifice at Olympia, tried to bribe Antipater's father to have the boy announced as a Syracusan. But Antipater scorned the tyrant's gift and announced that his family and he were from Miletus, and that he was the first Ionian to dedicate a statue at Olympia.

77   Pausanias VI.18.6   *ca.* A.D. 170
Lest we think that only the ancient Syracusans tried to "hire" a national team, the following passage is included.
When Sotades won the *dolichos* at the 99th Olympiad (*384 B.C.*) he was proclaimed as from Crete, as he actually was. But at the next

Olympiad he took a bribe from the Ephesians and announced that
he was from Ephesos. For this the Cretans punished him with exile.

78   Xenophanes, fragment 2   *ca.* 525 B.C.
*The poet and philosopher Xenophanes, in his arguments for the
values of intellectual accomplishments, shows that critics and
criticism of athletes and athletics were known long before the time of
Philostratos and Galen (above nos. 69 and 70), and even before the
glorification of athletes by Pindar (below nos. 81-83).*

Even if a man should win a victory in the sanctuary of Zeus at
Olympia in the foot races or the pentathlon or the wrestling or the
painful boxing or in the dreadful struggle which men call the
pankration, even if he should become a most glorious symbol for his
fellow citizens to observe, and win a front row seat at the games and
his meals at public expense (*see above, no. 74*) and some especially
valuable gift from the state, even if he should win in the horse races,
and even if he should accomplish all of these things and not just one
of them, he still would not be so valuable as I am. For my wisdom is
a better thing than the strength of men or of horses. The current
custom of honoring strength more than wisdom is neither proper nor
just. For the city-state is not a bit more law-abiding for having a
good boxer or a pentathlete or a wrestler or a fast runner even
though the running may be the most honored event in the games of
man. There is little joy for a state when an athlete wins at Olympia,
for he does not fill the state's coffers.

79   Euripides, *Autolykos,* frag. 282   *ca.* 420 B.C.
*The Athenian playwright Euripides, in this work of which we possess
only a fragment, carries on the attack against athletics a century
after Xenophanes.*

Of the thousands of evils which exist in Greece there is no greater
evil than the race of athletes. In the first place, they are incapable of
living, or of learning to live, properly. How can a man who is a slave
to his jaws and a servant to his belly acquire more wealth than his
father? Moreover, these athletes cannot bear poverty nor be of
service to their own fortunes. Since they have not formed good
habits, they face problems with difficulty. They glisten and gleam

like statues of the city-state itself when they are in their prime, but when bitter old age comes upon them they are like tattered and threadbare old rugs. For this I blame the custom of the Greeks who assemble to watch athletes and thus honor useless pleasures in order to have an excuse for a feast. What man has ever defended the city of his fathers by winning a crown for wrestling well or running fast or throwing a diskos far or planting an uppercut on the jaw of an opponent? Do men drive the enemy out of their fatherland by waging war with diskoi in their hands or by throwing punches through the line of shields? No one is so silly as to do this when he is standing before the steel of the enemy.

We ought rather to crown the good men and the wise men, and the reasonable man who leads the city-state well and the man who is just, and the man who leads us by his words to avoid evil deeds and battles and civil strife. These are the things which benefit every state and all the Greeks.

80   Thucydides V.49-50   420 B.C.
Thucydides here describes the situation when the Eleans excommunicated the Spartans from the festival at Olympia. It cannot be mere coincidence that, just before the Olympics of 420 B.C., Elis had concluded a treaty with Athens, Argos, and Mantinea against the Spartans.

During this summer there were the Olympics at which Androsthenes of Arcadia won his first victory in the pankration. The Lacedaimonians were excluded from the Sanctuary of Zeus by the Eleans so that they could neither sacrifice nor compete in the games. The Lacedaimonians refused to pay the fine which the Eleans had imposed upon them in accordance with Olympic law for allegedly breaking the Olympic truce. When the Lacedaemonians refused to pay the fine, the Eleans suggested that, since they were so eager to have access to the sanctuary, they should stand on the altar of Olympian Zeus and, in front of all the Greeks, swear that they would pay the fine later. Since the Lacedaimonians did not want to do this either, they were excluded from the sanctuary, the sacrifice and the contests, and sacrificed by themselves at home, while the rest of the Greeks sent delegations to the festival at Olympia. The Eleans were afraid that the Lacedaimonians might try to sacrifice at Olympia by force, and kept guard with their young men armed. About a thousand Argives, a like number of Mantineans, and some Athenian cavalry came to help them.

A great fear came over the festival that the Lacedaimonians would march under arms, especially when a Lacedaimonian, Lichas the son of Arkesilaos was flogged by the umpires because, when his team of horses won but was announced as belonging to the people of Boeotia because he had no right to compete, he had run up and crowned the charioteer so that he could make clear that the chariot was his. Thus everyone was in a great state of fear and it seemed that something was going to happen. But the Lacedaimonians kept their peace and the celebration was completed.

81   Pindar, *Olympian Ode* 7.1-16, 80-93   464 B.C.
During the first half of the fifth century B.C. the poet Pindar wrote dozens of odes in honor of victorious athletes at the panhellenic games. It is through his poetry more than any other single source that we form the usual picture of Classical Greek athletes and athletics. For some of the descendants of Diagoras of Rhodes, the honoree of this ode, see above, no. 35.

As when a man takes up in his wealthy hand
a drinking cup brimming with the dew of the vine,
and gives it to his new son-in-law,
toasting his move from one home to another
to the joy of his drinking companions
and in honor of his new alliance and thus makes him,
in the presence of his friends an object of envy
for the true love of his marriage bed;
Just so do I send my liquid nectar, gift of the Muses,
sweet fruit of my talent to the prize winners
and please the winners at Olympia and Pytho.
Truly blessed is he who is surrounded by constant good repute,
for the Grace who gives the bloom to life now favors one, then
    another
with both the sweet singing lyre and the variegated notes of the flute.
To the accompaniment of both have I now come
with Diagoras to his land while singing of
Rhodes, daughter of Aphrodite, bride of Apollo.
I have come to honor his fighting form and his skill in boxing
and the great man himself who was crowned by the Alpheios
and by the Kastalian spring, and to honor his father Damagetos.

Twice crowned with the laurel has been Diagoras,
and with his good fortune four times at famed Isthmia,
and again and again at Nemea and at rocky Athens.
Nor is he a stranger to the bronze shield at Argos,
nor to the prizes in Arcadia and at Thebes.
And he has won six times at Pellana and Aegina
while at Megara the stone tablet tells the same story.
O father Zeus, give honor to this hymn for a victor at Olympia,
and to his now famous *arete* in boxing.
Grant him grace and reverence among his townsfolk
and among foreigners.
He travels the straight path which despises *hubris*,
and he has learned well the righteous precepts of good forefathers.

82   Pindar, *Nemean Ode* V.1-11   485 B.C.
I am no sculptor who carves
statues doomed to stand on their bases.
I send forth on every merchant ship, on every mail boat,
my sweet song to speed from Aegina and announce that
stalwart Pytheas son of Lampon has won the crown
for the pankration at the Nemean Games.
And he still a lad showing on his cheeks a summer tan,
a delicate sign of youthful bloom.

83   Pindar, *Pythian Ode* VIII. 79-98   450 B.C.
In Megara you have a prize already, Aristomenes,
and in the plain of Marathon, and three victories
in Hera's games in your home of Aegina.
But now you fell heavily and from high and with malice aforethought
upon the bodies of three opponents.
For them there was at Delphi no decision
for a happy homecoming like yours,
nor did happy laughter awaken pleasure in them
as they ran home to their mothers.
They slunk through the back alleys, separately and furtively,
painfully stung by their loss.
But he who has won has a fresh beauty and

is all the more graceful for his high hopes
as he flies on the wings of his manly deeds
with his mind far above the pursuit of money.
The happiness of man grows only for a short time
and then falls again to the ground,
cut down by the grim reaper.
Creatures of a day, what is a man? what is he not?
Man is but a dream of a shadow.
But when a ray of sunshine comes as a gift from the gods,
a brilliant light settles on men,
and a gentle life.

84   Aristophanes, *Birds* 904-957   414 B.C.

*In this comedy, Peisthetairos and others begin a new kingdom of the
birds as a replacement for and an improvement upon the real world
ruled by men, but problems continue to appear. One of these is in
the form of an itinerant poet, and it is quite clear that Aristophanes
was thinking of Pindar and of others like him.*

PEISTHETAIROS: Let us pray as we sacrifice to the feathered
    gods.

POET: (enters singing): O my Muse, praise the blessed Cuckoo-
    cloudland, and hymn her fame in song.

PEISTHETAIROS: What in the world is this? Tell me, who are
    you?

POET: I am a sweet-tongued warbler, a song-bird and poor servant
    of the Muses.

PEISTHETAIROS: How can you be a slave and wear your
    hair so long?

POET: I am no slave, but all we teachers are poor servants of the
    Muses.

PEISTHETAIROS: Is that why your cloak is so shabby and poor?
    But tell me, poet, what ill wind has blown you here?

POET: I have been composing sweet songs and lovely poems to
    celebrate your Cuckoocloudland.

PEISTHETAIROS: You cannot have been composing such
    anthems. When did you begin?

POET: Long, long ago did I begin to sing the praises of this state.

PEISTHETAIROS: I have not yet celebrated the tenth day
    since the founding of this state.

POET: Ah, but the Rumor of the Muses is as swift as the flashing
feet of horses; but give to me whatever you choose willingly.

PEISTHETAIROS: He'll make trouble for us now unless we give
him something to get rid of him. Hey, you there, you have a
leather jacket and a chiton. Take off your jacket and give it to
this wise poet. Here, take the jacket; you do seem cold.

POET: This gift my Muse accepts
and not at all unwilling,
but turn your mind to learn
of Pindar's word fulfilling.

PEISTHETAIROS: Can't we get rid of this fellow?

POET: Through nomadic Skythia wanders Straton
with no undershirt to display,
Disgraced by jacket with no chiton.
Please perceive my point I pray.

PEISTHETAIROS: Sure. I perceive that you want the chiton too.
Hey, you, take it off. We have to help the poet. Here, poet,
take it and go away.

POET: (exiting): I am leaving, for I have made pretty songs for the
city.

PEISTHETAIROS: Thank God! This is an evil I never hoped for,
that he would find our city so soon.

85 Isocrates, *Antidosis* 166   353 B.C.

*At the age of eighty-two, the orator and political scientist Isocrates
lost a court case by the negative vote of an Athenian jury. Feeling
that he was generally misunderstood and not appreciated by his
fellow citizens, Isocrates wrote a self-justifying pamphlet in which he
included the following argument.*

It would be the height of absurdity if Pindar the poet was so
honored by our ancestors for the single line in which he called
Athens the bulwark of Greece that they made him a *proxenos* and
gave him a gift of $80,000, but I who have paid our city and our
forefathers much greater praise and written such beautiful eulogies
am not to be accorded the simple honor of living out my days in
peace.

*Isocrates and Aristophanes (above, no. 84) are both referring to the
same fact: Pindar (as well as other poets, artists, and sculptors) were*

paid for their works. Thus if we today are to view ancient athletics objectively, we must understand two principles. First, Pindar and others glorified athletes not merely because they thought that athletes were worthy of glorification, but also because they were paid to do so. Secondly, the athletes who commissioned these works had sufficient wealth to be able to pay for depictions, whether verbal or visual, of their arete. Some athletes will have inherited their wealth, but others, such as Theagenes of Thasos, clearly owed their financial status to their arete.

Appendix

I. The Events of the Olympic Games
and the
Date When Each Was Added to the Olympic Program

stadion	776 B.C.
diaulos	724 B.C.
dolichos	720 B.C.
pentathlon	708 B.C.
pale	708 B.C.
pyx	688 B.C.
tethrippon	680 B.C.
pankration	648 B.C.
keles	648 B.C.
stadion for boys	632 B.C.
pale for boys	632 B.C.
pentathlon for boys	628 B.C. (dropped immediately)
pyx for boys	616 B.C.
hoplites	520 B.C.
apene	500 B.C. (dropped in 444 B.C.)
kalpe	500 B.C. (dropped in 444 B.C.)
synoris	408 B.C.
salpinktes	396 B.C.
keryx	396 B.C.
tethrippon for foals	384 B.C.
synoris for foals	264 B.C.
keles for foals	256 B.C.
pankration for boys	200 B.C.

II. The Events of the Pythian Games
and the
Date When Each Was Added to the Pythian Program

kithara-singing	586 B.C.
aulos	586 B.C.
aulos-singing	586 B.C. (dropped immediately)
stadion	586 B.C.
diaulos	586 B.C.
dolichos	586 B.C.
pentathlon	586 B.C.
pale	586 B.C.
pyx	586 B.C.
pankration	586 B.C.
keles	586 B.C.
stadion for boys	586 B.C.
pentathlon for boys	586 B.C.
pyx for boys	586 B.C.
dolichos for boys	586 B.C.
diaulos for boys	586 B.C.
tethrippon	582 B.C.
kithara	558 B.C.
hoplites	498 B.C.
synoris	398 B.C.
tethrippon for foals	378 B.C.
pankration for boys	346 B.C.
synoris for foals	338 B.C.
keles for foals	314 B.C.

Index and Glossary

ageneios. Literally, "beardless," a term used to designate an age category for competitors between the category for boys and that for men. The specific age limits for the *ageneios* category varied from place to place, but were generally for the late teens. By the Hellenistic period, this category was in use for nearly all games including the Pythia, Isthmian, and Nemean, but it was never adopted at Olympia which retained the two basic categories of boys and men. 46, 84-85.

agonothetes (pl. *agonothetai*). The sponsor, producer, or manager of games. The *agonothetes* had general responsibility for the conduct and the smooth functioning of the games, and at times also for underwriting their finances. 57-58.

akon. A light spear or javelin. 8, 12-13, 15, 30, 46, 54, 72-73.

akoniti. Literally, "dustless," a term used to designate a victor who had won without a contest. This was usually the result of his opponents' physical or psychological incapacity to compete with him, and initially was used exclusively of the heavy events of wrestling, boxing, and the pankration. 60.

Alcibiades of Athens. 93.

Alexander the Great. 63-65.

Alpheios River. 29, 56, 97.

Altis. The sacred grove at Olympia, an area surrounding the Temple of Zeus, defined in the fourth century B.C. by a wall. In theory, everything within the *Altis* was sacred and all secular activities and buildings were kept outside this open square. 34, 58.

Anacharsis. 20-22, 42-44.

ankyle. (Latin: *amentum*) A rawhide thong, roughly six feet in length which was used in throwing the *akon.* The *ankyle* was doubled over and wrapped around the shaft of the javelin beginning with the two loose ends. The index and second finger of the thrower were inserted in the resulting loop of the *ankyle,* and the javelin held with the remaining fingers and thumb. During the throw, just after the instant of release, the javelin which had already received something like a sling-shot thrust from the *ankyle,* spun from the unwinding thong which dropped to the ground. The result was not only greater distance, but also a spiraling or rifling effect which stabilized the flight and the accuracy of the *akon.* 30.

Antipater of Miletus. 94.

Antiphon. 72-73.

apene. A wagon or cart drawn by mules and used for a relatively brief period as one of the equestrian events at Olympia. 102.

aphesis. Literally, a "letting go" or a "sending forth," used generically of the starting line for both the foot races and the horse races. 38, 39-40.

apodyterion. An undressing room, usually in a palaestra or gymnasium, where the athletes disrobed prior to practice. It is not clear where they disrobed prior to competition, but the tunnel entrances to the stadia at Olympia and Nemea are possibilities. 41.

Apollo. 3, 8, 12, 22, 31, 42, 57, 86, 88, 97.

aporrhaxis. the name of a ball game, apparently a sort of handball. 70.

archery. 12, 15.

Ares. 64.

arete. A word for which we have no simple equivalent in English. *Arete* includes the concepts of excellence, goodness, manliness, valor, nobility, and virtue. It existed, to some degree, in every ancient Greek and was, at the same time, a goal to be sought and reached for by every Greek. The best definition will be that formed by the reader who sees how ancient authors used the word. 1, 3, 15, 27, 44, 54, 68, 77, 87, 98, 101.

Aristophanes. 35-37, 99-100.

Aristotle. 73-75, 76-79.

Arrhachion (or Arrhichion) of Phigaleia. 27-30.

Astylos of Kroton (or Syracuse). 48, 49, 94.

Athena. 3, 4, 10, 15, 93.

Athenaeus. 63, 66.

Athens and Athenians. 16, 18, 44, 49, 50, 57, 72, 73-74, 94, 96, 98.

Argos and Argives. 1, 5, 8, 28, 48, 49, 50, 85, 96-97, 98.

aulos. Generally any wood-wind instrument, but usually and specifically a flute. Competitions in playing the *aulos* were a part of some festivals including those at Delphi, Isthmia, and Athens, but not at Olympia and Nemea. There were also competitions in singing to the accompaniment of the flute, *aulos*-singing, although this contest at Delphi was dropped immediately after its initial performance. 30, 45, 83, 97, 103.

balbis. An area in the stadium track marked off for the diskos throwers. Sometimes used generally of the starting line for the runners. 31.

bater. Generally, that which is tred upon, like a threshold. Used of the taking-off place for the *halma* and, more generally, for the starting line in the stadium.

boule. The council or senate in a city-state. The Olympic *boule* consisted of 50 Eleans who had general control over the Olympic festival. The meeting place of any *boule* was generally called the *bouleuterion.* 61, 74; cf. 47.

boxing. see *pyx.*

caestus. The boxing glove of Roman times. A leather strap wrapped around the hands and usually loaded or studded with pellets of lead or iron.

Chiron of Pellene. 63.

chlamys. A heavy cloak or mantle worn especially, but not exclusively, by cavalrymen. 74.

chrematitic. The adjective applied to games where the prizes were either of money or of monetary value as, for example, in the Panathenaic Games at Athens.

circus. Generally, the Latin word for circle, but usually the name for the oval horse race track in Roman times. The most famous of these was the *Circus Maximus* at Rome. 80, 84.

Corinth and Corinthians. 40, 48, 49, 50, 51-52.

dancing. To the extent that dancing was a part of athletics, it was military in nature and formed a part of the Ephebic training. 15, 46, 76, 80.

Delphi (see also Pythian Games). 20, 41, 42, 48, 57, 58, 59, 60, 62, 94, 98.

demes. These were territorial subdivisions of Attica and elsewhere. A township is the best modern analogy, and membership in a *demes* was a prerequisite to citizenship. 74.

Demeter. 41, 56.

Demokedes of Kroton. 91-93.

Diagoras of Rhodes. 56, 97-98.

diaulos. One of the footraces which was twice the *stadion* in length; that is, a sprint down and back the length of the track. 17, 38, 49, 71, 90, 102, 103.

didaskalos (pl. *didaskaloi*). Generally, a teacher, a master of any subject who trains his students in that subject. 74.

Dio Chrysostom. 51-53, 80-81.

Diodorus Siculus. 63-65.

Diogenes. 51-53.

Dionysia. 58.

Dionysios of Syracuse. 94.

Dioxippos of Athens. 63-65.

diskos (pl. *diskoi*). Originally a weight of unformed stone or metal which came to be shaped more or less like our discus and to have the same meaning in athletic contexts. In other contexts, *diskos* had the meaning of anything disc-shaped. 4, 11, 13, 14, 22, 30, 31, 35, 52, 58, 69, 89, 96.

dolichos. The only long-distance foot race. The absolute length is uncertain even at Olympia where the evidence is better than elsewhere, but it was probably 24 lengths of the stadium there, or nearly 5,000 m. 17, 49, 60, 65, 90, 102, 103.

elaiothesion, A room in a palaestra where athelete oiled themselves. 71.

Elis and Eleans. 20, 28, 29, 34, 40, 48, 53, 56, 57, 62, 87, 96.

ephebeion. A room or a recessed bay in a palaestra set aside for the use of the *epheboi.* 71.

ephebos (pl. *epheboi*). A young man who had reached the age (eighteen) of training for and ultimately entry to citizenship. His training was called ephebic (*ephebike*) and was vital to the state in the creation of a military reserve. 70, 73, 74.

episkyros. A type of ball game played by teams and vaguely resembling soccer or American football. 70.

Euripides. 89, 95-96.

Euthymos of Lokroi. 49, 59-60.

exedra (pl. *exedrai*). An architectural term for a large recess or a room with one wall open, usually with benches around it and common in palaestrai. 71

follis (diminutive *folliculus*). A type of ball invented in Roman times made of skin or bladder and inflated with air. 66.

frigidarium. The Latin term for the cold water bathing chamber within a bathing complex. 71.

Galen. 66-70, 87-91, 95.

gymnasion. The Greek word which yielded our gymnasium is literally the name of a place where nude exercises take place. Technically, it should be kept distinct from the palaestra although the two buildings were often physically connected. In this sense, the *gymnasion* consists of a covered practice track or *xystos* one *stadion* in length. Parallel to this, but in the open air, is the uncovered practice track or *paradromis.* Practice for the *akon* and the *diskos* will have taken place beyond the *paradromis.* 22, 41, 72, 73, 85. 87.

gymnastes (pl. *gymnastai*). Literally, a trainer of nude exercises, but the term came to have the specific meaning of a trainer or coach for a professional athlete. 79, 87, 89.

halma. Generally, any leap, spring or bounding, but specifically the jumping part of the pentathlon which resembled our broad jump with the additional use of the *halteres* and the accompaniment of the *aulos.* 13, 22, 30, 52, 69.

halter (pl. *halteres*). A small weight (usually about five pounds) shaped essentially like a dumbbell. A *halter* was held in each hand of the jumper and could, with careful coordination and rhythm, result in longer jumps than without the use of the *halter.* 30.

harpaston. The name of a ball game and of a relatively small stuffed leather ball. 66-72.

Hedea. 57.

Hellanodikes (pl. *Hellanodikai*). The name of the ten judges or umpires wo officiated at the Olympic Games. 27, 29, 39, 40, 51, 54, 56, 57, 59, 60.

hemerodromos. Literally, "running through the day," but used substantively of a courier, a messenger runner. 18.

Hera. 57.

Herakles. 18, 53, 60, 64, 90.

Herodes Atticus. 57.

Herodotus. 18, 50-51, 91-95.

Hieron of Syracuse. 49, 94.

himas (pl. *himantes*). An oxhide thong wrapped around the knuckles, wrist, and forearm to serve as a boxing glove. The earlier and more simple *himantes* were called "soft" to distinguish them from the "hard" *himantes* of the Hellenistic period which had protruding layers of leather which increased the protection for the wearer if not for his opponent. 9, 24, 26, 27, 28.

hippodrome. The track for the horse races. 39-40, 42, 55.

Hippokrates. 87, 88.

Homer. 1-15.

hoplites or *hoplitodromos*. The name of a foot race in armor which was like the *diaulos* in length. The competitors originally wore helmets and greaves on their shins, and carried shields. The greaves were later abandoned as part of the equipment. 17, 48-49, 65, 102, 103.

hubris. Wanton insolence, arrogance, the cause of many a man's downfall. 98.

hysplex (pl. *hyspleges*). The name of the mechanism or of the rope or gate part of the mechanism which was used for starting the foot and the horse races. 39.

iselasis. A driving into or an entrance. Used in Roman times for the triumphal entry by an athlete into his home town after a victory. 86.

Isocrates. 100.

Isthmia or Isthmian Games. 20, 40, 42, 43, 44, 48, 51-53, 57-58, 60, 84, 87, 94, 98.

javelin. see *akon*.

Julius Caesar. 80.

jumping. see *halma*.

Kallipateira of Rhodes. 56.

kalpe. This is the name of an equestrian event at Olympia for a brief period. The evidence indicates that it was either a race for mares, or a race which involved the rider jumping off and running along the horse for a part of the race. These two possibilities are not, of course, mutually exclusive. 102.

kampe. Literally, a bending or turning. Used of the general area where the turn was made in the foot and horse races, or of the turn itself. 40.

kampter (pl. *kampteres*). The name of the post where the turn was made in the foot races and the horse races. 42.

kanon (pl. *kanones*). Generally, any straight rod or stick, but sometimes a measuring stick or ruler of variable length. 35.

Kastalia. The name of a spring near Delphi. 97.

keles. A riding horse and the name of the horse-back race. The length seems to have been six laps, or twelve lengths, of the hippodrome. 39, 46, 48-49, 94, 102, 103.

keryx. Any herald, but including those who won the competition at Olympia and were rewarded with the honor of calling events and announcing victors. 54, 83, 102.

kithara. The harp or lyre. *Kithara* playing, as well as singing to the accompaniment of the *kithara,* was one of the competitive events at Delphi and Isthmia, and at many of the local festivals. 45, 82-83, 97, 103.

Kleomedes of Astypalaia. 59.

Kleonai. A small town a few miles east of Nemea which originally controlled the Nemean Games, but was ousted by Argos by the end of the fifth century B.C. 83.

konisterion. The room in a palaestra where athletes dusted themselves. 71.

korykion. A punching-bag room in the palaestra. 71.

Kosmetes. An official at Athens who was elected annually to be in general charge of the *ephebike* training. 74.

Kreugas of Epidamnos. 28.

Kyniska of Sparta. 56.

Lacedaimonia (see also Sparta). 16, 23, 29, 96-97.

laconicum. The sweating room, or "sauna," in a bathing establishment. 71.

lampadedromia. A torch race used as a part of civic and religious ceremonies and competed in by the different tribes of *epheboi.* 18, 47.

Leonidas of Rhodes. 17.

Lichas of Sparta. 97.

loutron. The name of a Greek bathing establishment, or of a bathing chamber within the palaestra. 71.

Lucian. 20-23, 42-44, 50-51, 53-55.

Marathon. One of the *demes* of Attica, site of the battle between the Athenians and the Persians in 490 B.C. The ancient battle of Marathon has absolutely nothing to do with our modern race of the same name which was invented in 1896. 18, 98.

Melancomas of Caria. 81.

meta (pl. *metae*). The equivalent in the Roman circus of the Greek *kampter.* 80.

Milo of Kroton. 51, 58, 93.

music (see also *aulos* and *kithara*). 13, 15, 61-62, 76, 78, 82-83.

Nemea or Nemean Games. 20, 28, 40, 42, 58, 60, 83, 84, 94, 98.

Nero. 81-83.

nyssa. A largely poetic (and especially Homeric) equivalent of *kampter*. 2, 10, 13, 40.

obsonia. Literally, foodstuffs, things eaten with bread. In Roman times the name of the pensions given to athletes who had won at a "Sacred Game" (so-called because the emperor had so-called it) after their celebration of an *iselasis*. 86.

odeion. Usually a building for musical performances. a recital hall. 41.

Olympia or Olympic Games. 16, 20, 27, 28-29, 34, 39-40, 42, 43, 47, 48-51, 53-55, 56-57, 58-61, 62, 63, 71, 79, 82, 83, 90, 93, 94, 95, 97-98, 102.

Orsippos of Megara. 16.

ourania. A ball game. 70.

paidagogos. Literally, "leader of the boy." A kind of tutor for a young boy, frequently a slave or servant who took the boy to school and home again. 38.

paidotribes (pl. *paidotribai*). Literally, a "smoother of the boy," or a "polisher of the boy." A trainer for physical activities including athletic exercises and military drills. 66, 69, 74, 79.

palaestra. The wrestling school (see also *gymnasion*). 71-72.

pale. The word for wrestling both as an event and as an exercise. The event was practiced with both competitors in an upright stance and with the objective of throwing the opponent to the ground. The winner was determined by the number of falls, probably three out of five. There were no time-limits, but delaying tactics as well as fouls were punished by a whipping from the judges. 7-8, 9-10, 13, 15, 18-23, 45-46, 48-49, 52, 58, 67, 76, 84-84, 95, 102, 103.

Pan. 18.

Panathenaia. The name of the local festival at Athens which was the largest and best known of the *chrematitic* festivals in Greece. 42. 44, 44-47.

pankration. The name for the "all-powerful" contest which was a combination of boxing and wrestling with no holds barred except for biting and gouging. Delaying tactics and fouls were treated as for the *pale*. The victor was determined by one of the opponents holding up an index finger to signal his own defeat. 20, 22, 23, 27-30, 32, 45-46, 49, 59-60, 62, 64, 75, 83, 84-85, 95, 102, 103.

ATHLETICS
OF THE
ANCIENT WORLD

By

E. NORMAN GARDINER, D.Litt.

With a Preface to the American Edition
By
PROF. STEPHEN G. MILLER
University of California
at Berkeley.

ISBN 0-89005-257-3.   xviii + 246pp + 64pl. $22.00

"Nearly half a century has passed since the original appearance of E. Norman Gardiner's *Athletics of the Ancient World.* In the interval many discoveries have been made which ought to have rendered Gardiner's work obsolete; many books have been written on the subject which ought to have replaced *Athletics of the Ancient World.* It has, however, not been replaced as is shown not only by this, but also by previous reprints in 1955, 1965, 1967, and 1971, all of which have sold out making the book once more unavailable. The principal reason for the continued usefulness of *AAW* lies with its author. E. Norman Gardiner was recognized during his own lifetime as the unrivaled authority on Greek Athletics . . . . . The timelessness of Gardiner's work lies, then, partly in his enormous learning. It lies even more, however, in his ability to write intelligibly for both the interested layman and the specialized scholar. The status of our knowledge is made clear, the source of information obvious, problems well defined, but never to the confusion of the reader. His learning sits gracefully upon his lucid prose, and one recognizes that Gardiner knew his subject matter intimately, cared for it tremendously, and wanted to share it generously."

From the *Preface* by Prof. Stephen Miller.

THE LIBRARY OF ANCIENT ATHLETICS

Knab, R. DIE PERIODONIKEN: Ein Beitrag zur Geschichte der gymnischen Agone an den 4 griechischen Haupt-festen.

[330-8] vii + 83 pp. $12.50

The *Periodonikai* or victors in the cycle (*periodos*) of the four Panhellenic festivals mark the beginning of professional athletics in the classical world. Particularly during the Roman Empire, they won widespread recognition both in the provinces and in Rome. Knab lists chronologically and alphabetically all the known *Periodonikai* from the 6th c. B.C. to 3rd c. A.D. References to all authors and inscriptions mentioning *Periodonikai* are included. (1934).

Klee, T. ZUR GESCHICHTE DER GYMNISCHEN AGONE AN GRIECHISCHEN FESTEN.

[336-7] 136 pp. $12.50

Klee's well known monograph on the Greek games and the festivals connected with them is heavily based upon the epigraphical evidence available before WWI. Despite this fact, however, his work is internationally recognized as one of the few major classics of the history of Greek athletics.

Robinson, R. SOURCES FOR THE HISTORY OF GREEK ATHLETICS.

[297-2] xii + 289 pp. $10.00

It has been a source of great satisfaction to me, on returning to my long-planned book on Greek athletics, to find that a need for it still exists. In the present edition three new chapters have been written: The Legendary Origins of Games at Olympia; The Rise of Organized Athletics; the Hellenistic Age. Many new translations have been added and representative evidence from inscriptions and papyri has now been included. The rather full notes seek not only to explain certain aspects of the translations but also to provide essential information for those who would investigate more deeply the many unresolved problems of athletic history.

SEXTUS JULIUS AFRICANUS. *LIST OF OLYMPIAN VICTORS.*
ΟΛΥΜΠΙΑΔΩΝ ΑΝΑΓΡΑΦΗ

Edidit *I.R. Rutgers.*
[351-0] [Leyden 1862] 8½ x 11 inch. Hardbound $25.00

The text of Sextus Julius Africanus, as edited by I.R. Rutgers, is an essential reference for the student of ancient Greek history and athletics.

Rutgers has produced an excellent critical edition of the Greek text, adding in footnotes all parallel texts of both Greek and Latin writers, and completing his work with a superb collection of testimonia of Olympian victors and victories not recorded by Sextus Julius Africanus. A detailed *Index-Nominum* makes the book a true *Prosopographia Olympionicarum;* a unique reference in which all available information on Olympian victors and their victories is recorded with every necessary detail.

This work is extremely rare; according to the *National Union Catalogue,* only three copies existed in the United States and Canada, previous to our printing. We do not know how long our edition will remain in print. To be sure that you secure a copy, order now, directly from the publisher.

Hyde, G. DE OLYMPIONICARUM STATUIS A PAUSANIA COMMEMORA-TIS.
[341-3] 80 pp. $15.00

Hyde's work is a superb study for anyone wishing to understand the relationship of the olympian victors to those whose names were inscribed on the bases of the statues observed by Pausanias when he visited Olympia in the second century A.D. The names from Pausanias' record and the inscriptions found upon bases excavated by archaeologists complete and verify the traditional list of the Olympian victors.

ARES PUBLISHERS Inc.
7020 NORTH WESTERN AVENUE
CHICAGO, ILLINOIS 60645

ORDER FORM

Author	Title	Price
		Total Books

THE ANCIENT WORLD $10.00 Per Four Issues
Postage and Handling Extra. *Minimum Charge $1.00*

TOTAL

Directions For Ordering and Payment

For Fast, Economical and Convenient service order directly from: John Corvin, Order Dept./Ares Publishers

Personal Checks on U.S. Banks only are accepted for payment of orders. Overseas customers please pay by check in U.S. Funds drawn on an American Bank or with an International Postal Money Order. Customers anywhere in the world may charge purchases to Visa Card or Master Charge Card.

Postage and Handling Extra. *Minimum Charge $1.00*

☐ VISA ⌊⌊⌊⌊⌋ ⌊⌊⌊⌋ ⌊⌊⌊⌋ ⌊⌊⌊⌋ Expiry ⌊⌊⌊⌋

☐ Master Charge ⌊⌊⌊⌊⌊⌊⌊⌊⌊⌊⌊⌊⌊⌊⌊⌋ Expiry ⌊⌊⌊⌋

Copy number above your name on ► Mastercharge ⌊⌊⌊⌋

☐ Signature _____

NAME _____

ADDRESS _____

PLEASE NOTE OUR NEW ADDRESS

ARES PUBLISHERS Inc.
7020 NORTH WESTERN AVENUE
CHICAGO, ILLINOIS 60645